MAKING MANAGERS

CHARLES HANDY · COLIN GORDON · IAN GOW ·
COLLIN RANDLESOME

PITMAN

PITMAN PUBLISHING
128 Long Acre, London WC2E 9AN

© Charles Handy, Colin Gordon, Ian Gow,
Collin Randlesome 1988

First published in Great Britain 1988

British Library Cataloguing in Publication Data
Making managers
  1. Managers. Training
  I. Handy, Charles B. (Charles Brian), 1932–
  658.4'07124

ISBN 0 273 02929 0 (Paperback)

Typeset by Avocet, Bicester, Oxon
Printed in Great Britain at The Bath Press, Avon

CONTENTS

ACKNOWLEDGEMENTS

This book had its origins in the study commissioned in Britain in 1986 by the National Economic Development Council, the Manpower Service Commission and the British Institute of Management. The study resulted in a report published in April 1987 under the title 'The Making of Managers'.* The authors are greatly indebted to these sponsors both for the opportunity to undertake the original study and for their permission to draw on it for this book. They are also grateful to Her Majesty's Stationery Office for their permission to quote substantial sections of the actual report.

Many people helped to make the study possible and to keep it true. Michael Moloney, on secondment from the Manpower Services Commission was an invaluable staff officer and co-ordinator for the project. Without him we should never have got to where we should have got, and never have pulled the bits together in time. Cyril Leach and Cecil Fudge of the Manpower Division of NEDO were assiduous in their support of the study, visited two of the countries with us, edited and checked the script of 'The Making of Managers' report as it materialized and offered wise comment on many matters. Without their constant help the report and therefore this book would not have happened. Cyril Leach, in addition, has contributed the case-studies in the American chapter of this book.

In the countries we visited there were a large number of people who most willingly answered our questions, opened their doors and introduced their colleagues. There is, unfortunately, no space to name them

* The report can be ordered from the National Economic Development Office Millbank Tower, Millbank, London SW1P 4QX.

all but we should like to thank particularly, Professor H. Okamoto of Hosei University in Japan, T. Werneck of Siemens AG in West Germany, Professor Dominique Xardel of ESSEC in France and Professor Lawrence McKibben of the University of Oklahoma in the USA who acted as our principal advisers on the original study. For Britain, Professor John Constable and Roger McCormick, whose report 'The Making of British Managers' was published on the same day as our report, provided a wealth of information and advice.

There is a long history of reports and writing on the education and development of managers in Britain. The authors owe a particular debt to some of them. Professor Thomas Kempner pointed the way for this book with his seminal article 'Education for Management in Five Countries: Myth and Reality' in the *Journal of General Management*, Winter 1983/84. Professor Reginald Revans, the architect of Action Learning has been the unseen, and too often unacknowledged, inspiration behind much of the best practice discovered in the study in Britan and elsewhere. Alistair Mant and Trevor Owen in their respective reports cast early doubts on the wisdom of placing too much reliance on classroom learning for the development of managers. Professor Iain Mangham, in his 1986 study of management training within companies, alerted us to what can only be called the sporadic nature of much of the present-day provision of training in British companies. The long list of other authors is provided in the bibliography.

The sponsors of the study did more than provide financial support. Sir John Cassels of NEDO, Geoffrey Holland of the MSC and Peter Benton of BIM have been generous with their time and their ideas. A roadshow, to introduce the findings of the study to a wider audience of business managers and teachers, was organized by the British Junior Chamber in four British cities in December 1987, with the support of the MSC and helped us significantly to improve our interpretation of our findings.

Material from the report *The Making of Managers*, HMSO, 1987, that appears throughout this text is reproduced with the permission of the Controller of Her Majesty's Stationery Office.

1 THE QUEST

BY CHARLES HANDY

It started early in 1986 in Britain.

'Go', they said, 'go and see how the others do it and come back and tell us if there is anything which we are missing and should be doing'.

'They' were the National Economic Development Council, the Manpower Services Commission and the British Institute of Management. 'It' was the whole process of educating, developing and training managers. 'The others' were our principal competitor countries – the USA, Japan, France and West Germany. The common concern of the sponsors was a worry that perhaps we were neglecting in Britain one of the key competitive factors, the quality of management.

In the end, of course, the brief was expressed more formally and more fully but those early words conveyed the gist of it. This book is an account of that journey and of our reflections upon it; 'we' in this case being the members of the study team and the joint authors of this book, picked for our knowledge of at least one of the countries to be visited, and of its language, as well as our personal involvement in management education and development.

The book is a fuller account than the one which the much briefer final report contained and the reflections are the richer as a result of the many discussions, debates and conferences that were one immediate result of the report's publication in April 1987. It would probably be true to say that in all these debates few people questioned or argued with the analysis in the report although there was, and continues to be, much discussion of the practical recommendations for Britain.

This book concentrates on the analysis in the belief that it is the underlying analysis which will be of continuing value and interest to a wide group of people, whatever eventually evolves in Britain itself. There is, however, a brief epilogue which outlines how Britain is developing its own approach, partly at least as a response to the report and to the parallel study on the British scene by John Constable and Roger McCormick.

THE FIRST QUESTIONS

There is a considerable amount of literature and information on the education, training and development of managers in each of the four countries visited and in Britain. Seldom, however, has it been compared and contrasted. A simple early desk study revealed some startling differences, best expressed as a series of questions:

– Why do 85 per cent of top managers in both the USA and Japan have university degrees, whilst the only available comparative figure in Britain suggests 24 per cent? (See Table 1.1.)

– Why are there over 120 000 qualified accountants working in Britain, but only 4000 in West Germany and 6000 in Japan? (See Table 1.1.)

– Why, on the other hand, does Britain graduate only 1200 British MBAs (Master of Business Administration) a year whilst the USA produces 70 000, West Germany none and Japan only 60? (See Table 1.1.)

– Why, however, do 54 per cent of the directors on the managements boards of West Germany's 100 largest companies have doctorates, not in management, but in some discipline such as engineering, science or law?

– Why do most well-educated West Germans not join a business until 27 years of age or later whilst the British and the Japanese start at 22?

– Why do the large corporations (2000 or more employees) in France spend 3.36 per cent of their wage bill, on average, on training when their law only requires 1.2 per cent?

– Why do 42 per cent of the top 300 companies in America and many big corporations in West Germany and Japan expect, even guarantee, to devote more than five days off-the-job training each year to every manager?

Table 1.1: Some statistical comparisons

Country	Top managers with degrees %	Numbers of qualified accountants 000s	MBAs per annum
Britain	24[1]	120.0[6]	1 200[7]
USA	85[2]	300.0 (est.)	70 000
West Germany	62[3]	3.8	0
France	65[4]	20.0 (est.)	0[8]
Japan	85[5]	6.0	60

Sources:
[1]Koudra, M, *Management training, practice and attitudes*, BIM Management Survey report, 1975; [2]Survey by Korn Ferry Int., 1986; [3]Evers, H. and G. Landsberg. *Qualifikation und Kariere* Deutsches Institut, 1982; [4]INSEE National Statistics Office; [5]Survey by Tokyo Keizai Magazine.

Notes:
[6]Accountants working in Britain – combined estimates of six professional bodies; [7] British nationals; [8]INSEAD graduates not included. It is not part of the French system.

– Why is a career in management so sought after in all four of the other countries but apparently less so in Britain?

– Why do so many Japanese companies need a formal manual for what they call on-the-job training (OJT)?

To some extent the differences lie in semantics; different countries have different names for the same things. The differences, however, go much deeper than words. This was the first lesson we were to learn. There is no common, well-understood, procedure for learning to be a manager. Management development, it seems, is not like science, unchanging in its laws and applications whatever the language, whatever the culture. Each country has its own way, rooted in its own educational historical traditions. On the other hand, weaving their way across the differences there are detectable similarities, similarities of principle, of emphasis and, we believed, similarities of new priorities and new urgencies.

Internationalism is one example; once the speciality of a few, it is now required of all aspiring managers. The ways, however, which one country will instinctively adopt to give its managers an understanding of internationalism will differ dramatically. To many Americans internationalism would become a 'required' and not an optional course on the curriculum of an MBA course or a special one-week seminar for senior managers at an organization's private school. The Japanese, on the other hand, would instinctively want to respond by sending their managers or would-be managers to work and study in another country. It would be much more expensive but much more effective, they believe.

The Europeans, perhaps because of their imperial past, still tend to assume that what works at home will work abroad. To the Germans this means that good technology is universal, to the French that rational calculation makes good sense in every language, to the British that character and common sense will pull you through in jungle or in desert. These long-held beliefs are changing, however. The Germans and the French realize that the habits, beliefs and preferences of individuals and societies do impinge on technology and on rationality and that, therefore, not everything can be pre-planned, pre-learnt and and pre-programmed. The British are realizing, on the other hand, that there *are* things which can be studied and learnt in a formal way, things which can complement the initiative and judgement of the individual.

These are crude stereotypes, of course. They are cited here to indicate how cultural and historical assumptions can affect the ways in which different countries think of the management role and of the proper preparation for it. Words and language are important, therefore, not in themselves but because they offer clues to those underlying assumptions and to the differences and similarities which we found to be so important.

THE DIFFERENCES

Americans put a high value on *education* in all aspects of life. If, as their history suggests, every American is responsible for his or her own destiny with nothing pre-determined at birth, then education has to be a sensible investment in one's future. It is fashionable in America to 'go back to school' in the corporation as much as in other walks of life.

Early in this century, American universities began to put management on a par with the traditional professions from an educational point of view. They created business schools modelled after law schools and sought to give these schools an equivalent status.

The result has been to give the manager in America a quasi-professional status in his or her role, a role typically prepared for in a professional way by study in academic surroundings leading to a university degree. One quarter of all undergraduates in America today are majoring in business studies and one quarter of all postgraduate students are studying for an MBA.

The zest for education as an investment in one's potential carries over into the larger companies, many of whom maintain their own 'corporate colleges' and most of whom make regular use of the executive programmes in universities as well as offering tuition reimbursement schemes for part-time study. Education is big news in corporate America.

The culture suggests that it is up to the individual to make the most of the opportunities available, both for education and for advancement. The big corporations plan these opportunities systematically; the smaller companies live in a more open market-place. The development philosophy of the typical large corporation is well summed up in the phrase 'individual initiative and corporate support'.

The *Japanese* are, as one might suspect, very different culturally. Intelligence is greatly respected, but the job of managing can, they believe, only be learnt by watching, listening to, and practising under one's older and more experienced colleagues. On-the-job-training (OJT) is a Japanese maxim.

To this philosophy must be added the tradition, particularly in the large corporations, of lifetime employment and a steady progression up the seniority ladder. Given the prevalence of such a tradition, there is no need for external credentials, no urgency to acquire experience, no need to stand out as an individual. It is slow-burn development.

As a result, Japan has only one, small, American-style business school. Potential managers are recruited direct from university into the corporations. There is keen competition for entry into a way of life which guarantees security, advancement and eventual high status. The potential manager then embarks on a period of apprenticeship which can last for up to 14 years. The apprenticeship consists of a mix of specific jobs, often across a range of functions, combined with formal instruction in company practices, discussions with colleagues and superiors, external correspondence courses in business or related areas, occasional essays and frequent formal reviews. OJT in Japan is a formal, regulated and planned pattern of development, appropriate to a culture which claims to know where it and you are going and to take a large measure of responsibility for getting you there.

The *French* are different again. The intellectual tradition in France is a rationalist one, heavily influenced by the predominance of mathematics in all French schooling. The legal tradition is Napoleonic, set down by decree from the centre, rather than by accumulating case-law and precedent.

Given these twin traditions, it should be no surprise to find that the French response to a perennial need for more training in companies some years back was to pass a law requiring every business to spend at least 1.2 per cent of its wage bill on training or forfeit it to the Treasury. The law further required every company to prepare a development plan for its personnel and to allow a period of paid leave to any employee who wanted to spend time in further education. The law also insisted that companies produce annual statistics on training and these statistics demonstrate that the minimum requirements of the law are normally exceeded by factors of two or three in most of the larger companies.

Prior to this law it was often tacitly assumed that the regular influx of some of the best brains in France from the *grandes écoles* of business and engineering would be enough to restock the management echelons with the right material.

It has long been an important part of the French tradition that business should have its proper share of the intellectual élite, not least because this gave management a status equivalent to the professions and government. There is, however, today a growing recognition that management is more than pure rationality and that a small élite, often working in specialist roles, is not enough.

The *Germans* in West Germany have another tradition and another culture. It is one of thoroughness and relevance, finding expression at one level in their widely admired schemes of apprenticeship and, more generally, in the theories of their educational philosopher Wilhelm von Humboldt who argued that his country should 'teach them long, teach them broad and teach them in large numbers' – no room here for a rationalist élite.

Management in West Germany is predominantly functional management, the supervision of those less skilled and experienced by one more so. General management is a title reserved for the top, while 'management' as a concept on its own, divorced from what is to be managed, is not widely understood or accepted.

The aspiring manager in West Germany, therefore, is well advised to find an apprenticeship in some relevant industry after leaving school and before joining a university where he, and it is still typically he, will study some relevant discipline such as science, engineering, law or economics for up to seven years, and even longer if he wants a doctorate, as many do. The humanities are not thought to be a relevant field of study for would-be managers. Add to all those years the period spent by most young males in military or community service and it is no surprise to find that most well-educated Germans are 27 or more before they start their first job.

After entering the larger companies an individual's development is planned, usually within a particular function. Career moves are integrated with relevant training in a carefully systematic way. Thoroughness and relevance are taken seriously by young and old alike.

The *British* belong to none of these traditions. To the British management has always been a more of a practical art than an applied science. It is a word moreover with a rather lowly pedigree; to 'manage' in colloquial English usage means usually to 'cope', whilst 'manager' was traditionally a title reserved for the more mundane service functions ('transport manager', 'catering manager') rather than for the senior roles in an organization.

Given this tradition and those beliefs, it made some sense to rely primarily on a Darwinian system of development; meaning that the effective manager would emerge and the ineffective would be weeded out in the light of experience. Character, initiative, energy and imagination have always been more important words in the British managerial tradition than knowledge or intellect.

The gradual emergence since the Second World War of management as a career and as a quasi-professional role in British society led to a variety of experiments in the training and preparation of would-be managers. A few big organizations went the Japanese way, recruiting management trainees from the universities with the intention of providing them with an appropriate mix of training and experience throughout their career. A few, principally in the City, emulated the French in going for the brightest and then leaving them to get on with it with little or no further training. Some universities and more polytechnics sought to transplant the American tradition of formal study into Britain, although after more than twenty years of effort the numbers of graduates are still small. There was even the well-known attempt to copy the tradition of the Services by founding an Administrative Staff College at Henley. Nobody copied the Germans.

None of these efforts, however, succeeded half so well as the attempt, perhaps unconscious, by the accountancy profession to professionalize business. It is, in our view, no accident that Britain has 168 000 accountants on its registers with 120 000 working in Britain, whereas Japan has only 6000 and East Germany less than 4000. These accountants in Britain are, for the most part, not auditors, they are in business – as managers, as consultants, as staff specialists. Accountancy is, for many young Britons the accepted professional route into business. If ten per cent of all British undergraduates aspire to be accountants it is not because they want to be auditors but because they want to be business men and women.

The individual countries are each dealt with in much more detail in the separate country chapters. The key features are outlined here only in order to emphasize that any approach to the education, training and development of managers *has* to take into account the historical and cultural context. There is no one right way to do it.

THE SIMILARITIES

Despite the very obvious differences, there were some clear similarities, particularly between the four other countries. There were also some pointers to the future, because none of the countries was completely satisfied that its ways were necessarily the right ways for the years and the problems ahead.

1   In all countries it is the large corporations which set the pattern. They may, in total, only employ about 20 per cent of the work-force but they produce a disproportionate amount of the wealth, they are the principal customers and suppliers of small business and they are, whether they

want to be or not, the breeding grounds for many of the managers of small businesses, new and old.

What they do therefore matters nationally. The smaller businesses have to work to their standards. To some extent, the smaller will always feed off and poach from the larger. Inevitably, therefore, the larger companies are the research laboratories and the business schools of the society. They should not shirk this role and in Japan, particularly, they do not. In France and Germany some of these obligations are channelled through the Chambers of Commerce which are primarily training organizations financed by business subscription and used extensively by small as well as big organizations.

2   In the four other countries, it was particularly noticeable that 'the beginnings are crucial'. The educational infrastructure not only provides an important base for would-be managers to build on but also goes a long way towards guaranteeing a work-force with the aptitudes and skills needed in modern business. Each of the four countries visited did, in its different way, set out to make sure that a large proportion of young people got a broad education to at least 18 and that a significant percentage then stayed on for university studies. Britain was exceptional in this regard. (See Table 1.2).

As a result, the other countries have a bigger pool of well-educated young people from which to select their potential managers, avoiding the excessive competition for the few which drives up starting salaries and has, in Britain, helped to exclude large sectors of business from participating in the recruitment of this educated minority. The other countries can also expect their new recruits to be in their middle or late twenties (except in Japan where a continuing education programme is part of the early years in a company) with a variety of educational and work experiences behind them (including military service in France and West Germany).

It is noticeable, as a result, that many more top managers in the other countries had had a university education than is the case in Britain (85 per cent in the USA and 62 per cent in West Germany, for example, versus 24 per cent in Britain. See Table 1.1). Not only, then, are these managers likely to be more predisposed towards education but they are themselves establishing a pattern for the young. It is probably not a coincidence that in the two countries which have the highest proportion of university-

Table 1.2: Participation rates in education

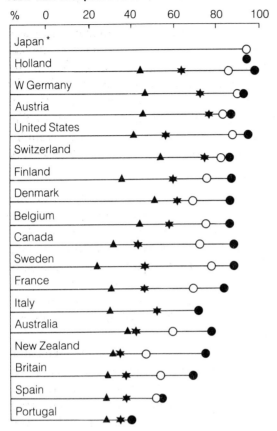

Aged: ●16 yrs   O17 yrs   ✹18 yrs   ▲19 yrs

* Not all figures available

Reprinted with permission from *The Economist*.

educated managers (the USA and Japan) business and industry are both highly regarded and careers in them prized by the aspiring young. There is no anti-intellectual culture in business in the other four countries; there has been, at least until recently, in Britain.

3   A good education is a necessary prelude to a successful career in management but, by general consent, it does not stop there. Further education, training and development is a conscious policy in the leading corporations in all five countries. They differ mainly in the ways they organize it. In Japan and in Germany it is very formalized, particularly in

the larger organizations. In the USA, France and Britain it is more opportunistic – what Adam Mumford has pleasingly called 'accidental development'[1]. A written statement of policy, often expressed diagrammatically, was usually available on request in the large organizations in the other countries, infrequently in Britain[1].

There is a consistent belief in all countries that self-development is the key to learning, tested and grounded in experience at work. The difference again lies in the degree to which this belief is carried forward into policies and procedures. In their different ways Japan and the USA are noticeable for their insistence on what Japan called 'self-enlightenment' and the USA 'individual initiative', both backed by corporate support. In the other countries self-development might be expected but is seldom formally encouraged.

4   Looking to the future it seems, in all countries, that the idea of a 'cadre' or separate group of people designated as managers and trained early on for management is no longer thought desirable. Most people will increasingly start work as specialists and acquire, often very soon, responsibilities for project supervision or people or money or all three but would remain operators as well as managers.

A parallel trend is the demise of the 'middle-manager' and the flattening of organization structures, a trend which again tends to make more people part-time managers and to push business accountabilities down the line and across specializations.

One consequence of this is the need for more people to know the rudiments of business and to acquire the skills of management. Business and management education will become an almost universal requirement as the whole work-force becomes more skilled and more autonomous.

A second consequence is the inevitable compression of career ladders which will probably force more and more people into the external managerial labour markets. Flat organizations can offer variety and achievement but not promotion.

More individuals will be looking for credentials to support their track record. More training and educational programmes will be expected to count for credit against some qualification. This is likely to be true even in Japan where it is estimated that only a small proportion of today's entering graduate class will be appointed *kacho* or first-level manager because the jobs will not be there. There are already head-hunters in Tokyo in the financial services sector.

THE GENERAL CONCLUSIONS

As a result of our quest there were certain general but important conclusions to be drawn. Although with hindsight they are, perhaps, rather obvious, they need to be stated because it is only by starting from these conclusions that a coherent set of proposals for action can be developed. The one that we proposed for Britain is set out at the end of the chapter on Britain.

1   There needs to be a clearly understood pathway to becoming a competent manager. The process of *formation*, to use the French word, needs to be recognized by employers and aspiring managers and to be adopted by the majority of large employers.

This pathway should, however, be appropriate to the traditions of the culture and to its educational infrastructure. No one country can or should ever be a perfect model for another.

2   There is a clear distinction to be made between *business education* and *management development*. Both are important and interlinked but they are different.

Business education is to a large extent the responsibility of the individual. A basic business education (learning the languages of business) should be required of every aspiring manager and was, in the other countries, expected of them either before entry or soon after entry. It is usually provided by an external source (university course, business school or correspondence college) and paid for by the individual or, occasionally, by the organization. Individuals will sensibly up-date their business education by reading and occasional courses throughout their working life.

Management development is a mixture of experience, training and education which is usually initiated by the organization with the necessary co-operation of the individual. Much of it takes place within the organization although experts can be imported to help with the training and education and individuals can be seconded to other organizations or to business schools and executive training courses. The training and education is related to current or immediate next jobs and assumes at least as much benefit to the organization as to the individual.

Business education is a relatively long-term study, involving some eight or nine different fields of knowledge and the acquisition of some basic analytical and processing skills. It cannot easily be compressed into one or two weeks as part of a management development programme.

On the other hand, a business education is not, by itself, a qualification for management, only a prelude to it. You cannot learn enough about the real-life dilemmas and skills of managing by studying the problems of business and management in a classroom.

A proper process of formation will include provision for both business education and management development almost certainly handled and delivered in different ways by different institutions.

3   All the education and training in the world will make little difference if the individual is not in a position to try it out. The best incentive to learn, we realized, is to be in a situation where you are concerned that your responsibility might exceed your competence. Early responsibility, high expectations and standards and every facility and encouragement to study or learn from others proved to be a potent combination for high achievement and high morale. The best organizations in every country used this combination, sometimes because they had to in fast developing markets or sectors (e.g. the financial services or consultancy). A culture which demands a lot from individuals will also look for the best and be able to afford to pay them well. In this day and age many of the best will have automatically attended university and will be looking for a career which combines opportunity for advancement with opportunity for further education and training. The culture, in other words, is self-fertilizing.

Education and training, therefore, need a development philosophy in order to be fully effective.

4   Smaller companies are different. In no country do they take the same long-term view of management development, nor are they prepared to spend the time and the money on any form of education or training which does not have an almost immediate pay-off. In an increasingly complex world, there is a real chance that they will get left behind. It is in the interest of everyone to make it easier for them to study and to learn. The Chambers of Commerce in France, and Germany and Japan are training organizations, on a regional basis, largely financed by the bigger

companies but geared to short-term business needs. They are a useful model but more needs to be done to bring learning to the individual in the work-place and in his or her home. This should be a major opportunity for distance learning.

5   There is more than one way to learn. All countries use traditional learning practices involving teaching and practice, formal study and formal examinations (Japan is perhaps more traditional than most). But each country also recognizes that there are other forms of learning which are as important, if not more so. America has exported its case studies, its business games and management exercises. Japan has elevated the mentor role into a formal requirement of every manager. In Japan, too, they recognize that watching and listening to others can open one's eyes to new possibilities; they therefore encourage subordinates to sit in on discussions among their superiors, they avidly study their competitors, both on paper and on site, they routinely expose their own ideas to everyone concerned before coming to any decision. Britain has contributed the concept of action-learning, originally formulated in Belgium by Professor Revans[2] but since then widely imitated and adapted. It is based on the idea that managers learn best by finding real solutions to real problems in the company of friendly peers who use each other as a 'set' of consultants. Germany has cultivated the model of apprenticeship and France the science of rational analysis.

This variety of approaches only emphasizes that management requires a wide range of knowledge and an even wider set of skills. These skills have been usefully classified many years ago under three headings: *technical, human* and *conceptual*[3]. All these are necessary, particularly as one gets more senior. Technical skills (including those of analysis) can be learnt in relatively conventional ways, taught and then practised under supervision; human skills must be learnt rather than taught, preferably with help from some sort of mentor, and conceptual skills developed by constant practice stimulated by reading, observation and argument. The study made it clear that the different cultures have their preferences but also that, in an ideal world, all are necessary.

These five conclusions should be the basis for any national strategy for improving the quality of management. That there should be a national strategy, we have no doubt. That it should take into account the present and the past is clear. We now believe that there are important lessons to learn from other countries but that no country in itself offers an ideal model for any other.

Most people in most countries now perceive management to be a complex, difficult and challenging task. It can, most would agree, no longer be left to common sense and character. Young people in particular accept that there are things they need to learn, skills and aptitudes they should develop. They are prepared to invest in themselves. Corporations should do likewise. Governments should help to set the framework so that the many different bits of the education and training jigsaw can fit together to form a complete picture. Governments need, too, to ensure that the educational infrastructure is adequate and appropriate. It has to be a time of great opportunity, not only for Britain but for many others who may also have left 'management' to chance or 'accidental development' far too long.

2 JAPAN

BY IAN GOW

INTRODUCTION

Japan's amazing postwar recovery, her emergence as an economic superpower and her efforts to achieve major status as a leading technological and scientific nation have all contributed to a veritable boom in literature purporting to describe or even explain the 'Japanese Miracle'. This focus, in turn was primarily aimed at identifying the key factors contributing to Japan's tremendous competitiveness in world manufacturing markets since the mid-sixties. It is ironic that many of the elements being identified were, in the early postwar period, dismissed by both Japanese and Western scholars as premodern, inefficient, exploitative and unsuited for use by 'advanced' industrial nations. Those same elements, government–industry relations, management–labour relations, subcontracting, etc, are now offered up as panaceas for Western industrial nations struggling to retain or regain industrial competitiveness. This has generated a new body of literature concerned with 'learning from Japan' in order to compete or co-operate with Japanese industry in our respective domestic markets and in third markets. This development in management studies has been motivated, one has to say, more by the fear and desperation of Western executives, often searching for 'quick fix' solutions rather than from an innate drive to study best practice everywhere. There is clearly a shift in attitudes towards industrial Japan which reflects, in part, a continuing propensity for Western opinion on Japan to switch, suddenly and often wildly from one extreme to the other. Admiration, envy and awe can (and did even in the prewar period) quickly change to contempt and fear and vice versa. However, it is also true that changed attitudes also reflect new developments within Japan due to structural changes in Japanese industry such as those created by the two major 'oil shocks' of the 1970s.

It should, however, be borne in mind that the extant English language literature does scant justice to the diversity of management practices within Japan. In particular there are vast differences, in all aspects of management – including management education – between Japan's giant corporations and the dynamic medium-sized firms on the one hand and between these larger firms and the numerous and varied small and very small firms. Moreover one must also bear in mind the quite significant differences in management style and management development between firms in one industry and between industrial sectors. For example the problems and solutions for management differ quite markedly in 'sunrise' and 'sunset' industries. One should also be cautious about assuming that Japanese management and by extension, elements of management education, are a, if not the, secret of Japan's success. There is, so far, no clear evidence that Japanese management, however defined, is the key factor or even the most important factor in Japan's competitiveness in overseas markets in the postwar period. At best we can say that good managers, and indeed well-thought-out management development and worker training and development programmes may be a necessary but not sufficient factor for high productivity and success overseas. Again, however, it is extremely difficult to trace causal linkages between successful firms and excellent management education systems, in other words which came first? One might therefore begin by considering certain other factors which deserve attention in any evaluation of the postwar Japanese success story.

KEY FACTORS

Most attempts at analysing Japan's remarkable recovery after the Second World War would mention some of the following as instrumental in assisting that development. Japan was placed under an Allied (American-dominated) Occupation from 1945–52. The USA, initially, did not attempt to assist recovery due to a fear of revived Japanese militarism. However, the intensification of the 'cold war' changed that, and the Americans set about assisting Japan to reconstruct a strong economy. Since this had to be achieved after Japan was stripped of her empire, the emphasis had to be on a value-added, export-oriented economy. The USA poured in economic aid, in the form of funds, equipment and management and technical expertise. In addition, the USA pressured Japan's former enemies in Europe to open their markets and also opened her own to Japanese exports. This assistance was allied to the advantages of being a late developer, 'pursuer' nation whereby Japan concentrated on licensing technologies rather than on financing major basic research and development programmes. This, of course, built on an approach which had already been used in the prewar period. Stripped of empire, Japan's planners well knew that a standard of living above that of Third World neighbours was only possible if the nation gathered its resources in a most effective way and generated something akin to a 'war economy' mentality to engender a totally and continuously committed and obedient working populace. Again, as in the prewar period, Japan focused tremendous resources on education to provide the highly educated and trained work-force required for economic growth and success. Long-range planning has always been a key factor in Japanese development in the modern period. Based on a banking system designed specifically to assist rapid, forced development, Japanese corporate planners, operating relatively free from shareholder pressure, have been able to plan longer-term strategies for economic success at home and abroad. Japan has also been able to pursue economic growth without the burden of major defence expenditure. Although Japan ranks seventh in terms of overall defence expenditure, she has managed to keep costs to around 1 per cent of GNP since the mid-seventies. The allocation of expenditure to civilian and particularly applied R & D, based heavily on imported technological knowledge, has been carried out in competition with the USA which, ironically, has shouldered the major burden for Japan's defence. Comparative labour costs have not, since the mid-sixties, been seen as a major factor in Japan's continuing success, although the low wages of Japanese subcontractors, subsidiaries and suppliers still merit consideration. Sheer competitiveness in overseas markets must also relate to the position which exists domestically. The image of Japanese firms co-operating or 'colluding', seeking a consensus to achieve planned growth does not actually accord with the facts. Japan has probably the most competitive domestic market in the world, a fact often ignored by inadequately prepared Western firms trying to penetrate it. Japan has over close to 30 000 bankruptcies a year and the competition for market share is vicious. For example, in a corporate culture where enterprise (single firm) unions exist, when one of Japan's eight domestic car firms (or a similar number of camera or TV/Hi-Fi firms) goes on strike, the others do not come out in sympathy but increase production to capture market share. No Japanese firm ventures overseas without a continual and concerned backward glance at the domestic market. Indeed certain firms have found the domestic market so tough, in terms of moving up to the first division, that they have adopted an overseas first strategy to succeed against domestic competition. Arguably Sony and Honda are the best examples. In the past the domestic market was heavily protected, giving the Japanese time to develop competitive goods for export but today only informal barriers remain as Japan accelerates liberalization under increased trade-related pressures from the Western industrial nations.

The unique nature of Japanese government–industry relations has been seen as a key strength, in other words management of the economy. This can be seen as negative in the use of such terms as 'Japan Inc.' and 'bureaucratic-industrial complex', or positive in terms such as 'strategic industrial policy' and the like. There exists in Japan a complex interrelationship between a highly trained industry-oriented bureaucracy and big business, operating within a stable political environment namely the Liberal Democratic Party. This 'conservative' party has been in power for virtually the entire postwar period and merits serious consideration especially in terms of fostering the development of big business. It is now increasingly fashionable to downplay the role of government in postwar Japanese economic development but there is evidence of considerable intervention and control in the immediate postwar years. As we shall see later this applied particularly to measures and organizations designed to improve management education and productivity.

One would also have to consider the 'Japanese-style' enterprise itself. The concept of the enterprise as the community, operated under a form of managerial familism has often been used to explain Japan's success. In this type of firm, to quote Professor Robert Ballon, 'capital serves labour rather than the reverse'. A 1981 survey of the presidents of the 100 top firms by the *Nihon Keizai Shinbun*, their equivalent of the *Financial Times*, asked 'who does the enterprise belong to?' Sixty-six per cent replied that it belonged to 'management, the workers and the shareholders' whilst only 18 per cent stated 'shareholders' alone. This implies that company members are perceived as coming before shareholders for most top managers. Indeed, irrespective of the legal position, shareholders are regarded as little better than 'moneylenders'. The continuity of the enterprise, rather than short-term profit, is often claimed to be the main driving force behind such organizations where workers (regular workers that is) are described in terms of being members rather than employees. Although the picture is an ideal one, nevertheless it is certainly true that the recruitment and development of a homogeneous work-force is seen as a major strength. However, terms such as 'familism', in the Japanese context, are susceptible to differing interpretations. One should be aware that the 'family' concept in Japan can be based on a hierarchical authoritarian *samurai* tradition or a peasant-type interdependent one. It should also be pointed out, especially in the context of this report, that these large companies, until comparatively recently, operated with a core and peripheral work-force. The latter, comprising temporary, part-time, seasonal and day labourers, do not receive the same privileges, care and training as the core 'regular' or 'permanent' white and blue collar work-force and would not be regarded as part of the corporate 'family'. Increasingly, as peripheral work-forces have been trimmed due to the loss of employment opportunities through the introduction of microelectronics and 'mechatronics' as well as increased overseas production, the peripheral labour force has been shifted into the small and medium-sized enterprise, especially the subcontracting sector.

The groupism of Japanese society is reflected also in the interrelationships between enterprises in Japan, for it is the large corporate groupings rather than big firms *per se* which best reflect the unique nature of Japanese company life. The prewar family-owned combines (*zaibatsu*) have been succeeded by large-scale horizontal enterprise groupings (*kigyo shudan*) and vertically integrated enterprise groupings (*keiretsu*). These provide a complexity of networks and ties which are mystifying to most Westerners and indeed evaluations of their effectiveness, profit measurement, etc., are still areas of heated debate amongst Japanese scholars. These corporate groupings may well provide a major competitive edge. However, it is worth noting here that Japan's success, especially in manufacturing terms, has been to no small extent due to the existence of a dual economy whereby a myriad of subcontractors, subsidiaries and suppliers operate under conditions far removed from the idealized large firm environment so commonly described in Western literature. Japan's small and medium-size (SME) sector, larger than any other in the world, contains more than 99 per cent of all enterprises in the secondary and tertiary sector as well as 81 per cent of the work-force. It also has a very high number of bankruptcies (nearly 30 000 per annum). Although the start-up rate is also high, this figure does indicate cut-throat competitiveness and inefficiencies rather than the consensus-dominated, highly efficient Japanese industrial world so popular in English language accounts of Japanese business practice.

Nevertheless the Western image of Japan as an extremely well-managed industrial nation persists. In particular, Japanese-style management (*nihonteki keiei*) at the macro and micro-level has generated a tremendous interest in the West and one cannot deny that Japan does have a number of extremely well-managed firms. This report, however, does not have, as its principal focus 'Japanese-style management' but rather 'Japanese managers', who they are, and how they are created and/or developed. Some comments on Japanese-style management may be useful prior to focusing on the development of Japanese managers.

JAPANESE-STYLE MANAGEMENT

Over the last few years there has been a veritable deluge of writing about Japanese-style management, much of it journalistic, impressionistic and often consultant-driven. The idea that Westerners, usually with no knowledge of the language and no experience in Japanese companies, can identify and have identified the key elements in Japanese management has caused much amusement amongst Japanese scholars. They, despite their linguistic and other advantages, have so far achieved no consensus on whether there is a distinct entity called 'Japanese-style management', let alone that one can identify its key elements and even attempt to transfer them. Nevertheless, there is a conventional wisdom in the West on the subject and the following are representative of the key elements often cited:

Internal labour markets
Enterprise (single-company) unions
Seniority wage and promotion systems
Lifetime employment

Long-term planning perspectives
Bottom-up consensus decisionmaking
Extensive on-the-job training (OJT)
Range of company incentives (bonuses, etc.)

More recently quality control circles and just-in-time production management techniques have been added to this list. In fact the Western literature offers us a static, oversimplistic stereotype which merely reflects some of the elements of large firms in Japan. It fails to take into account company cultures and changed circumstances. In addition, even within large firms one would have to add qualifications to almost all the above factors. It is, for example, often omitted that a dual labour market of core and peripheral workers exists within such larger firms which has often led to discrimination, particularly against women.

There is a heavier dependence by manufacturing companies on subcontractors in comparison to their Western competitors. Indeed the vast proportion of Japanese companies are small and medium-sized enterprises which possess none of the above elements of so-called Japanese management. Very small enterprises (*reisai kigyo*) with less than 20 employees (manufacturing) or 5 (commerce and service) have 79.2 per cent of the number of business establishments and 32.9 per cent of the total work-force respectively. In manufacturing SMEs have 99.2 per cent of the business establishments, 71.9 per cent of employees and a 51.4 per cent share of consignments with 55.9 per cent of value added. There are further distinctions depending on sector. Many of these firms do not have either the resources or time to develop managers, and indeed managerial functions are often carried out by the owner/proprieter. His/her main managerial concern is often on the 'successor' problem once he/she cannot continue to manage alone.

There is no doubt that large and medium-size Japanese firms do spend considerable amounts on human resource development and appear to be managed by a highly educated and well-trained management cadre. The following figures, based on a major survey of 669 companies by the Nihon Sangyo Kunren Kyokai (hereafter JIVTA – Japan Industrial and Vocational Training Association) published in 1985 indicated a clear trend towards the establishment of education and training units in Japanese companies over the last decade. For example the number without specialist staff decreased from 38.7 per cent (1970) to 17.2 per cent (1985), the number with specialized departments almost trebled 7.1 per cent (1970) to 18.9 per cent (1985). Specialist sections increased from 31.9 per cent to 54.9 per cent in that same period. This is a considerable increase in the establishment of larger education/training departments with those headed by senior middle management (*bucho*) have doubled whilst those headed by junior middle management (*kacho*) have increased by almost 17 per cent. Before turning to the Japanese manager we must mention Japan's education system.

The Japanese education system

Japan has one of the most effective education systems in the world. Initially, building on Confucian principles and, from 1870, the needs of a modern industrial state, the Japanese developed a dual track (popular and élite) system in the prewar period. This was subjected to major reforms during the Occupation of Japan (1945–52) under American tutelage. The dual track system was replaced by a single track 6–3–3 (elementary/middle/high school) system followed by either 2 or 4-year universities. The principle of coeducation was introduced and there were major efforts at decentralization. However, since that time, the Ministry of Education has gained considerably more control over the system than Occupation planners first envisioned.

The first nine years are compulsory (from age 6) and paid for by the state. However all post-15 education is paid for by parents, whether in state or private institutions. Competition is fierce at all levels of education and the motivation of children, dedication and status of teachers, are all high. Competition, often referred to as *Shiken Shigoku* (examination hell) is now permeating down even into the pre-school kindergarten sector as parents, from all walks of life, make considerable sacrifices to ensure the best possible opportunity for success in the system. Parents also spend considerable amounts on *Juku* (private tutoring school) at all levels. Japan also has an extensive correspondence course system, including broadcast correspondence courses at secondary, high and university plus post-experience levels, and these courses can be for formal school courses or vocational. Nevertheless, although in many respects egalitarian, Japan's system is essentially a 'one-shot system' although one can of course obtain qualifications later in life. However, the internal labour market system operated by large élite firms in Japan (who tend to recruit from a small, but expanding, group of top universities anyway) would offer few opportunities for late starters.

In April 1985 93.8 per cent of middle school students entered senior high schools or technical colleges whilst 38.2 per cent (37.6 to 2/4-year universities). The 2-year colleges (termed *Tanki Daigaku* – short-term universities) predominantly accept women students (329 000 out of 366 000) whilst the universities have a larger proportion of male students (1 320 000 out of 1 734 000 – 1985 figures). Japan has, currently 460 universities (including 2-year colleges) of which 95 are national, 34 public and 331 private. Fees for private universities are higher than for national/public universities, thus intensifying competition for places at the latter which are often ranked higher in status terms. The top universities are Tokyo and Kyoto with a cluster just below them such as Hitotsubashi, Keio, Waseda, etc., and although Japan's business, political and bureaucratic élites have tended to come from Tokyo and Kyoto (Todai and Kyodai) the situation is changing, especially with industry, in terms of recruitment for management. Moreover there is now developing a new kind of university, the so-called industrial university, such as the Toyota Techological Institute or the Daiei (a large department store chain) University of Distribution Sciences.

The Japanese pump most of their funding into the primary and secondary system and it is worth considering the fact that, since over 93 per cent are staying on in the system until around 18, Japanese managers are actually managing a work-force which has significantly longer, wider and possibly more thorough educational training than other advanced industrial societies. Certainly the curriculum leans heavily on traditional skills, the 3 Rs and tends to be broader in terms of subject areas than, say, in England. Japanese children have a longer academic year than British children, including Saturday morning school, and we saw numerous weekend organized school trips whilst in Japan. Moreover the curriculum, whilst not as standardized as in the prewar period, is relatively uniform throughout the country and is based on the 'Course of Study' prepared and published by the Ministry of Education. There is, in addition a central government approved set of textbooks from which courses must be taught. However, local/regional government has the major responsibility for administration of the schools system in terms of appointment of teachers, etc. There is an ongoing dispute between the (left wing) teacher's union Nikkyoso and the Ministry of Education over textbook content, control of the curriculum, etc., with the teachers perceiving increasing central control as evidence of a reversion to prewar norms.

Universities tend to be more theoretical/academic than Westerners imagine although research has so far been skewed towards applications rather than fundamental R & D. Entrance exams demand a reasonably high level of skills across a wide range of subjects including compulsory mathematics, Japanese and a foreign language. Moreover, in a four-year degree course the first two years are more general with specialization occurring in year three. There is a tendency to see universities as geared to the needs of industry. Whilst, in general terms, higher education planning reflects the needs of an advanced industrial society, many industrialists especially in large firms, complain that they have to train new graduate recruits from scratch. Indeed, until very recently, co-operation between industry and the universities, especially in the area of applications, R & D was severely limited by red tape and the government is now trying to foster greater collaboration between industry, government and academia, the so-called Sankangaku policy.

There has certainly been a major expansion in business studies teaching, and many private universities boast departments or faculties of business administration, although the national universities have not adopted this approach. Graduates in business studies were deemed increasingly attractive by the firms we interviewed in Japan, especially those firms in the service sector, and there are indications of further shifts in the direction of vocationally oriented higher education especially in the private establishments. However, the development of postgraduate business schools on the Harvard model seems unlikely with only Keio effectively offering this type of education. The Ministry of Education is now considering how to design an effective system of 'lifelong education' to cope with changes in the industrial structure, rapid ageing of the Japanese population and the possible erosion of the lifetime employment system in the larger firms. In other words, mobility is now to be coped with and indeed, in many circumstances, to be encouraged, this necessitating continual retraining and re-education opportunities, if not a major shift towards a credential society. Whilst the Japanese educational system has its critics, there can be little doubt that it has proven 'functional' in meeting Japan's needs until now. Again, however, the needs of a 'pursuer' nation are considered by many, inside and outside of Japan, incompatible with Japan's new position as a 'pioneer' nation aiming for technological and scientific superpower status in the 1990s and beyond. Former Prime Minister Nakasone, during his period of office as well as others initiated investigations into curriculum reform, etc., which they hope may help them to develop a system more attuned to the needs of creativity.

THE JAPANESE MANAGER

Little, however, has been written specifically about the development of 'Japanese managers' other than often crude syntheses of translated materials provided by management organizations, large companies, etc., for visiting Western businessmen and academics. It is a well-known fact that foreigners often find great difficulty in clarifying the titles, roles and functions of Japanese managers. In part this reflects problems of translation and the use of British, European and American nomenclature in the translated titles. In part, it also reflects the difficulties of classification especially in a country where clear job specifications are uncommon. Nevertheless the following terms seem to cover the areas reasonably well.

Top Management	*Keiei kanbu*	Executives
Middle Management	*Kanrisha/midoru manejimento* *Chukan kanrishoku*	Middle management
	Bucho	Department chief/head
	Kacho	Section chief/head)
Junior Management	*Kakaricho*	Sub-section chief
	Daichisen kantokusha	First line supervisors
	Shokucho	Foreman
	Hancho	Group leader
	Uribasekininsha	Floor manager
	Shunin	Person in charge
	Tencho	Person in charge (store chief)

Terminology aside, the development and characteristics required for these positions differs according to company size and of course type of business. It is difficult to extract precise figures for the number of managers within Japan but according to the Management and Coordination Agency managerial employees occupied 8.1 per cent of the working population (0.8 female) in 1983. There would seem to be almost universal support in Japan for the assertion that middle management, however defined, is the real nucleus of the business team possessing long-term perspectives and dedicated to drafting plans for top management. Regarding key characteristics of Japanese managers, the following seem worthy of note and comprise the 'conventional wisdom' subject to certain qualifications.

1   Managers come from *within* the company, at least in the large and medium-sized firms where an internal labour market system dominates. Lateral entry in all but temporary/urgent skill shortage areas has, in the past, been discouraged. There is some evidence of change in the newly deregulated financial sector, however, and recent announcements by older established companies engaging in 'headhunting' have produced a rash of suggestions that the old system is crumbling. However, it may well be that such companies as banks moving into security business and security companies moving into banking are merely resorting to a temporary lateral entry philosophy as they have always done.

2   There is an almost complete domination of the management cadre in Japan by university graduates. This, however, fails to account for figures in the 1985 White Paper on Small and Medium-Sized Enterprises which intimates that only around 11 per cent of SME Presidents are university graduates. Statements about a graduate management cadre must therefore be carefully qualified although basically, like many other generalizations on Japanese management and managers, it is truer the larger the company. Workers with only a senior high school diploma have, in the past, often made successful managers but these days rarely climb higher than the lower rungs of junior management. Professor Kagono has suggested that there are two types, university graduates reaching management positions after 5-15 years and non-graduates with 15-35 years of service. The latter grouping, a vestige of immediate postwar developments, is gradually disappearing as this generation retires. The graduate manager situation is reinforced by postwar education reforms resulting in more Japanese students entering higher education than in any other country except the United States. But the trend towards graduates in top management had appeared even before

the Second World War according to Japanese business historians. At the turn of the century Aonuma estimated 4.4 per cent of company presidents were graduates rising to an estimated 14.4 per cent just before the First World War according to Professor Morikawa. By 1928 the figure had reached an incredible 75 per cent. Professor Aonuma found that in 1960 top management graduated from university was Japan (90 per cent) USA (60 per cent) and UK (25 per cent). By 1975, *Toyo Keizai* magazine estimated that 85 per cent of top management were graduates according to a survey of 1681 listed companies.

One should, however, exercise some caution in assuming complete compatibility between Japanese and UK (or other national) statistic figures for graduates. Prewar Japanese figures are based on higher education including institutions which became universities after the Second World War. Moreover with over 460 Japanese universities at present, one might be sceptical of the comparability of those institutions at the lower end with higher education in the UK. Nevertheless Japanese managers, being graduates, have all had 15–16 years' formal education. Top Japanese management also, in the past, has tended to be dominated by graduates from a few élite state and private universities such as Tokyo, Kyoto, Hitosubashi, Waseda, Keio and Tokyo Technology Institute.

3   There is an almost complete absence of postgraduate business degrees and the extent to which professional associations award their own qualifications for use in a business context is limited. In a business environment attuned to lifetime employment and therefore low inter-firm mobility (in large firms anyway), it is perhaps logical that businesses should not place a high value on external qualifications which they, perhaps rightly, associate with overmobility, Western style. Japan is, as yet, a long way from being a credential society in terms of individual credentials; rather it is the enterprise affiliation which counts most of all. The number of Japanese taking overseas MBAs is, however, increasing and this trend, usually associated with international divisions of companies, will intensify as Japan focuses more attention and resources on internationalization.

4   The Ministry of International Trade and Industry (MITI) Industrial Policy Bureau in 1988 produced figures for large and dynamic medium-sized manufacturing enterprises (*Chuken Kigyo*) indicating that 35.2 per

cent of all middle managers did not have subordinates. The existence of rank and status promotion in the past has enabled around 60 per cent of graduate entrants to achieve management positions but recent estimates indicate that this rate will probably be halved in the very near future.

5   Managers generally tend to remain in the enterprise union until around section chief level (kacho) and after that they lose overtime payments and instead may receive managerial responsibility payments.

6   Wage differentials have been reduced considerably. The Japan Federation of Employers in 1982 stated that salary differentials between company presidents and freshmen (male university graduates) on entry were as follows:

1927	Pretax	110	times
	After tax	100.7	
1963	Pretax	23.6	
	After tax	11.9	
1973	Pretax	19.0	
	After tax	9.0	
1980	Pretax	14.5	
	After tax	7.52	

However, apparently such low differentials appear to be more common in the larger firms rather than SMEs where differentials are often considerably higher. The differences between lower middle management (kacho) salary (and bonus) and general employees have also been drastically reduced. According to Professor Amaya, a leading specialist in the area of management development, in 1935 managers received 10 times the salary and almost 25 times the bonus of general employees. In the early 1950s, in great part due to the economic democratization measures by the Americans, the differences were 3.1 and 6.7 respectively and today, on terms of both basic salary and bonus the average lower middle manager gets only twice the amounts of the general employees. Whilst Amaya's figures have not gone unchallenged the general trend indicated in his figures is undoubtedly correct. Compared to Western business practice, Japanese remuneration for management seems more egalitarian in nature reflecting to some extent postwar business reforms of the Occupation period (1945–52).

7   So far as the age structure of Japanese managers is concerned, long-term assessment and seniority based promotion have been the predominant practice up till now. This has created a situation where normally managers are older than all their subordinates and promotion is of the 'slow burn' type rather than the fast track, early talent spotting methods more common in the West. Junior management (*kakaricho*) is normally at 32, and middle management's section chief (*kacho*) at around 38 with department chief (*bucho*) around 43. We saw in Japan, however, that in certain industries such as the fashion company 'world' younger managers would appear.

RECRUITMENT

As a nation so bereft of natural resources Japan has, not surprisingly, always been willing to plough tremendous resources into developing the one resource she has in abundance, namely people. This is shown at its clearest in general education whereby over 90 per cent of children graduate from high school and 35 per cent go on to university. It is well known that the traditional Japanese practice in terms of blue/white collar core staff has been to recruit straight from university or middle and senior high school. Lateral entry or mid-career entry, whilst not unknown, especially in shortage areas such as cad/cam planning, etc., is typical in a business structure where the perceived norm is an internal labour market. Mobility is, of course, statistically relevant in Japan but given the high annual bankruptcy rate in the SME sector this is essentially involuntary mobility and can be discounted, although SMEs have been more likely to take trained, mid-career entrants than the larger firms. The 'enterprise as a community' concept means that extremely careful screening of a work-force with no previous work record is the norm in larger firms. This screening/selection process utilizes a far wider range of aptitude and psychological tests as well as check-ups with family, teachers, etc., than is the norm in the West. Increasingly the core work-force has come to be dominated by senior high school students for blue collar and graduates for white collar positions. Personality, ability to get on in groups, are usually regarded as more important than outstanding individual talent in selection although ability is, of course, still regarded as very important.

Competition for places in the top companies (everyone knows the rankings for each industry) is fierce both for recruiters and recruits. Starting salaries between industries appear to be almost identical and initial wage differentials stem from differences in school education with graduates at present receiving approximately 20 000 yen a month more than high school graduates. Women do receive similar salaries at the beginning but this tends to drop during the career. Japanese companies place a tremendous amount of emphasis on recruitment and induction training in order to achieve a honogeneous work-force and this has proved eminently suited to slow, incremental change. Shared backgrounds, shared values especially in terms of easing dissemination of the company's mission are relatively effectively achieved with a work-force which has, hitherto, assumed it would be with one company for life. Considerable expenditure on recruiting is therefore possible and very necessary given the long-term perspective in hiring core staff. Having thus carefully selected their human resource (a classic case of 'get it right first time') Japanese companies then expend considerable and continuing efforts to develop that resource over the entire career of the worker. Indeed a large number of companies actually commence forms of training even prior to induction training. This pre-employment training can consist of anything from newsletters/brochures about the company to specific short projects to be completed prior to joining the firm on April 1 annually.

EDUCATION/TRAINING

Given a mutual commitment to lifetime employment with the company – on behalf of employer and employed – training and education are seen as vital. Moreover, although it is generally accepted that the Japanese education system in general has been designed to produce a highly educated work-force, this education is general and not vocational, thus requiring companies to expend considerable effort and money on teaching basic business skills. The larger the firm the more is spent on training. Figures for training are notoriously difficult to obtain especially in view of the predominance of systematic OJT within Japanese companies at all levels. It is clear though the percentage of expenditure per worker drops off dramatically as company size decreases.

On the job training (OJT)

Initial training for all employees, graduate and non-graduate, normally comprises extensive induction courses followed by OJT and job rotation and these can be said to be the nucleus of early training programmes. It would, however, be misleading to assume that OJT was only used at the early stage since surveys indicate that it is continually used even for training and development of top management. In recent years surveys in Japan have continually referred to systematized/structured OJT and indicate that much more thought has gone into designing, implementing and evaluating the effectiveness of OJT programmes by superiors and trainers/educators within the firm. Essentially OJT comprises 'someone who possesses knowledge teaching one who lacks that knowledge'. Japanese managers, in the main, are much more inclined to be in favour of and keen to carry out the teaching and training of subordinates. One reason for this may be the very high esteem in which teachers are held in Japan. This in turn may reflect Confucianist attitudes or more pragmatic later developer traits. Again, in a system where a 'fast track' promotion system does not exist, people who pass on their knowledge are more secure sensing that their 'students' will seldom be promoted ahead of them at least until very late in their careers if at all. In OJT training in Japan the OJT trainer is not necessarily one's immediate superior. It could be an 'old hand' or even a specialized OJT trainer. These trainers in turn are taught either by in-company OJT counsellors or attend courses in OJT at peak management associations such as the Japan Management Association (JMA), Nippon Administrative Management Association (NOMA) or the Japan Industrial and Vocational Training Association (JIVTA). In management areas the practice of assigning someone to aid in this OJT system often seems close to the 'mentor' style of training now coming back into fashion in the West.

Often the training department will bolster work-place OJT by providing extra coaching when necessary. They are certainly active in providing OJT trainers, helping to set OJT policy through questionnaires to managers, etc., and also compiling detailed work procedure manuals. It is certainly not unusual for training departments to request a detailed report from line management on OJT development in their areas of responsibility.

Although systematic and structured OJT would more likely occur in larger firms it is also used quite extensively in smaller firms and especially in those with high technology levels. In one interview when the president of a small company was asked if there was such a thing as an OJT manual he replied 'Of course. We designed our own and it is given to all new employees'. However OJT is not used simply for ordinary workers, it is used extensively at all levels of management. Company-wide OJT objectives as well as OJT audits by training/education units and the use and development of OJT counsellors ensure that this method of training goes far beyond 'sitting beside Nelly'. Learning through experience (*taiken kyoiku*) is central to the OJT approach.

The Japanese tendency to favour open office planning for all workers up to middle management (*bucho*) levels clearly allows potential managers to observe their superiors, especially under stress, and is invaluable OJT experience. Moreover the elaborate systems of pre-consulation (*nemawashi*) prior to formal decisionmaking (*ringi*) are also excellent OJT skills for managers, and perhaps emphasize that consensus on problem definition rather than on solution is a much more effective approach to management problems. Once a consensus has been reached on a definition of the problem then a solution is often easier and certainly implementation of an agreed solution to a commonly perceived problem seems both sensible and effective. A generally agreed set of characteristic elements of OJT for Japanese management and supervisory staff has been provided by JIVTA. In their recent survey a large number of firms (669 replies) were asked to select four of the following as the most important. The results were as follows:

OJT Categories	Managers	Supervisors
1 Setting guidelines for development	47.7	27.7
2 Coaching for achieving objectives	44.7	41.7
3 Designing plan for development	37.2	28.6
4 Promotion of small group activities	33.6	48.4
5 Thoroughness of follow through	37.2	39.2
6 Evaluation of effectiveness	32.6	27.5
7 Fixed period interview and guidance	29.1	25.6
8 Delegation of authority	20.9	10.9
9 Improving job assignment	15.1	15.8
10 Assignment of specific tasks (reports, etc.)	10.8	5.1
11 Conducting problem-solving meetings	14.2	14.5
12 Encouraging self-control based on job execution standards	10.0	10.6
13 Job redesign	4.9	4.9

(*JIVTA 1985 Survey*, p. 36)

Disparities by scale of firm are relevant here and categories 1 and 3 are particularly emphasized by larger firms with their longer-term horizons on human resource development, whilst the short-term perspectives of SMEs are reflected in the popularity of 2. Differences also appear according to sector whereby secondary sector OJT emphasizes 7 and tertiary sector firms stress 2 and 5. Ultra-large firms in both sectors also emphasize 11 (30 per cent). At the supervisor level 4 is very important followed by 2 and 5.

Job rotation

A key element in OJT is job rotation, a practice much favoured by Japanese companies and of course vital in an internal labour market situation. It is particularly difficult, as with OJT, to estimate costs for this element of training. In an internal labour market the advantages of OJT in terms of development of competent generalists, information integration, networking and skill acquisition as well as peer and colleague assessment are tremendous. In terms of middle management, MITI's survey indicated that job rotation ranked fourth at 48.3 per cent behind external lectures, company residential courses, and management by objectives through self-assessment in large/medium-sized firms. Moreover, as can be seen from enclosure 5, this percentage is rising.

Japanese managers counter the Western criticism that job rotation is inefficient by stating that such a conclusion is based on a purely short-term measurement. They would argue that, over the medium and long term, job rotation enhances knowledge of the organization and expands one's networks. Moreover, whilst one might argue also that experience gained within one firm is very limited, Japanese managers can and do obtain wide experience by being job rotated to other companies in the group including subsidiaries and subcontractors. Japanese personnel departments also use extensive job rotation as a kind of horizontal fast track for potential 'high flyers'.

Off the job training (Off JT)

The image of Japanese firms being heavily dependent on company-specific on-the-job training is still a very powerful one. However, it is clear that there are also tremendous efforts expended on education and training away from the work-place. Indeed the literature on Japanese management education and development continually emphasizes that OJT alone is inadequate and must be complemented by systematic and sustained off the job training and development throughout the career of managers at all levels. Moreover this off the job training (Off-JT) increases the higher one moves up the company. The Japanese term *kenshuu* is also used and generally refers to in-house classroom-based learning. According to the 1985 SME Agency White Paper, 40 per cent of SMEs do not carry out Off-JT whereas only 3.5 per cent of firms with more than 399 employees (large firms) are not involved in such training. One further consideration is that Off-JT can, and often does, include training away from the company as opposed to away from the job.

Particularly important in the Off-JT area are efforts by individuals in acquiring further knowledge/skills by self-education/enlightenment at their own expense or assisted and encouraged by the company. Surveys show that insight and foresight are the main qualities required by department chiefs with almost no weight given to this at the junior middle management (section chief) level. Rather planning ability/creativity and specialist knowledge/skills were highly rated and increasing. Another method of looking at the qualities is to examine efforts to spot management potential early. In spite of the common assumption (confirmed by our interviews) that a fast track did not exist, there is

Methods of early management recruitment

Method	1978	1982
Observation and recommendation by superior	69.3	60.5
Aptitude test	28.6	28.2
Self-evaluation	43.2	43.5
Special assignment	20.6	10.2
Provision of instructors	3.0	2.8
Job rotation	33.2	26.0
Multi-source personal evaluation	38.2	40.1
Assessment programme	8.5	13.0
Evaluation through education	17.6	19.8
'Challenge' promotion system	5.5	5.1
Other	1.0	4.5

(Nippon Recruit Centre Shoshin Shokaku Jittai Chosa 1982)

evidence in a 1982 Nippon Recruit Centre survey of not inconsiderable efforts to detect management potential early on. Around 40 per cent of firms favour early management at selection with around 20 per cent actually carrying it out. This does not, however, imply necessarily a fast track if one sees that only in terms of upward mobility. Traditionally Japanese firms have rewarded rising stars by lateral promotion, that is by rotating them through an even larger number of jobs than is the norm. In terms of the actual training/development of middle managers the most popular methods were assistance with external courses/correspondence courses, residential courses for own staff, then management by objectives through self-assessment. In recent years, the major increases have been seen in residential company courses, job rotation system for ability enhancement, and salary increases/promotion reflecting acquisition of skills/qualifications. In addition, the establishment of organizations to study/plan/promote skill development and despatching managers to Japanese or overseas educational institutions or to other organizations has also increased. A recent MITI Survey found a marked correlation with high employee morale for companies scoring high on 4 or 5 of these areas.

As to the actual content of education, the following are the major subject areas for top and middle management in descending order:

1 Socio-domestic situation overseas
2 Corporation objectives/management planning/management strategy/management in general
3 Personnel/organization management
4 Stability in industrial relations
5 Voluntary initiative
6 Training and development of subordinates
7 Problem identification/solving
8 Ability to communicate
9 Creativity/development
10 International awareness
11 New technologies
12 Skill acquisition and development
13 Sales and sales management
14 Accounting
15 OA and Computerization

16 Vitalization of shop/organization
17 Corporate identity/image
18 Mental health

Interviews intimated a shift to emphasizing conceptual skills at all levels. In terms of development of management staff, a number of differences appear in terms of the most popular measures adopted. For top management and senior middle management, by far the most popular are external courses, seminars and study meetings, whilst for junior middle management in-company training courses appear the most popular with external courses only a few per cent behind. However at all levels of management over half the companies surveyed by JIVTA gave self-development/self-enlightenment as very important with a staggering increase in the last five years (1983–88).

Self-development

Self-development runs parallel with OJT and is being increasingly emphasized at all levels. In their most recent study, JIVTA added two new categories to self-education methods, namely 'supply of specialist knowledge and technology information' and 'assistance with obtaining official certificate'. The increased importance of the latter category may indicate an acceleration towards a 'credential society' and 'portability' of qualifications.

As for those most popular at present they are 'introduction of outside seminars and courses' 'assistance with expenses for individual development re correspondence courses, etc.', 'distribution of book lists' and 'assistance in obtaining official qualifications', and these were carried out in almost half the companies surveyed. If we compare this with the 1975 survey, significant increases are to be found in 'assistance with expenses for individual development re correspondence courses, etc.', and 'distribution of book lists'. Conversely, decreases are evident in 'assistance for voluntary study groups' and 'voluntary in-house courses'. Interview counselling for self-assessment has also decreased, but this seems to mean that companies are now carrying this out as part of the OJT system. Apart from that application ratios are not high but the 'in-house essay contest' system has also increased.

Measures designed to help with self-development naturally differ according to the level of employee targeted and also the scale of firm (and sector). Whilst SMEs also use 'introduction to outside seminars courses' and 'supply of specialist knowledge and technological data' albeit in slightly lower percentages, 'voluntary in-house courses', 'counselling for self-assessment' and 'in-house essay contests are much less used. Again 'in-company essay contests' seem much more popular in secondary industries than in the tertiary sector.

Self-Enlightenment/Self-Education

1 Distribution of book lists
2 Introduction of outside courses and seminars
3 Grants for individual study including correspondence
4 Assistance in obtaining official certificate
5 Information on specialist matters and technology
6 Counselling interview re self-assessment
7 Voluntary in-house courses
8 In-house essay contests
9 Assistance for voluntary study groups

A -2 -15

A 2 14 Changes in Promotion of and Assistance with Self-Education 1975–85

A Recommendation/introduction of outside courses and seminars
B Assistance with expenses for correspondence courses, etc.
C Counselling interview re self-assessment
D Distribution of book lists
E Assistance for voluntary study groups
F Voluntary in-house courses
G In-house essay contests
H Information on specialist matters and technology
I   Assistance in obtaining official certificate

An important element in self-development is the reading habits of businessmen in Japan. First there are the newspapers and in business terms the so-called 'industrial newspapers'. There are at least three major daily general industrial newspapers as well as the equivalent of the *Financial Times*. In addition there are numerous specialist newspapers for each industry, many of them dailies. Indeed, in terms of newspapers and journals Japan is probably the most well-read nation in the world. Japanese managers are extremely well read when it comes to books and magazines, including (and especially) business-related publications in foreign languages. If one adds to this the tremendous gathering, analysis and dissemination of domestic and foreign information by Japanese government and private organizations and industry associations, Japanese managers are extremely well informed and up to date. Indeed one of the fundamental differences between the average Japanese and the average British manager may be simply the managerial intellectualism and voracious reading habits of the former as compared to the attitude that 'I will only read it if its on 1 or 2 sides of A4' mentality of the latter.

Correspondence courses are extremely popular in Japan and these are often approved by the Ministry of Education. All the top management associations in Japan run correspondence courses of one kind or another and the companies are quite happy to provide financial support for these, fully or partially, and often pay on successful completion. One source listed as many as 3000 providers of business-related courses of this kind in Japan, but the main providers are the professional management associations. The Japan Management Association for example has just launched a new correspondence course for top management whilst the Nippon Administrative Management Association (NOMA) already runs a range of courses and estimates that in the Kobe/Osaka region alone some 20 000 managers are taking courses. There are also specialist organizations devoted to correspondence courses such as the Japan Management School (JMS) and the leading providers are Sanno University's Management Institute, Japan Management Association, Nippon Administrative Management Association, Japan Management School and Nihon Manpower. The type of materials offered, however, seems rather traditional with little use of modern distance-learning techniques. These, however, are now being studied. NOMA, for example, does not use a tutor system although students may ask NOMA staff for assistance with problems.

In-company group training

Surveys and interviews confirmed that lectures/addresses were still the most used teaching method in firms but there has been a large increase over the last five years in the 'group discussion/meeting method' especially for section chiefs. There has been a shift from 'grid/PM' type training and 'business simulation gaming' and an increased emphasis on 'in basket/case studies', especially the studying of actual examples of problems, etc. This tendency is again most marked at the section chief level (junior middle management). Methods of assessing the efficacy of such training naturally vary but there is growing evidence of a shift to written, detailed reports.

The most popular teaching staff (around 60 per cent) at all levels of company for these types of training were specialists from external specialist organizations. However, a high percentage (over 45 per cent) of companies also make extensive use of internal executives for lecturing, etc., for middle management training. Over the last five years there has been a significant drop in the number of lecturers from universities/ research institutions and in particular the use of visiting celebrities has dropped by almost 50 per cent. In-company training staff use ratios drop off quite sharply for teaching those above lower middle management (30 per cent).

Pre-promotion training

One area which was not sufficiently well answered during interviews but is clearly of immense significance is the nature of training/ development programmes prior to promotion, especially for senior management positions. Top management use ratios and categories were:

Job rotation and OJT after deployment	59.3(%)
Devising of measures relating to staff candidate training or qualifying exams	35.7
Enabling candidates to obtain wide management and staff experience in related companies	28.1
Career development programmes for potential top management	13.0
Carrying out from as early as possible assessments, career development programmes, etc.	16.1
Long-term despatch to domestic and foreign universities research establishments and other places outside the company	21.1

Development of abilities by simulations, business games case
    studies   27.5
Establishment of young executive committees   6.2
Placing them in charge of special projects.   21.7

These figures are based on a base of 100 for the 48.4 per cent of firms
surveyed actually stating they were carrying out such measures.
Regarding pre-training for promotion to management in general the
JIVTA survey calculated that approximately 28 per cent were carrying it
out with another 42.3 per cent wishing to do so. Clearly this listing refers
to formal OJT/off-JT but it is clear that considerable encouragement is
also given to candidates to participate in self-development programmes
with assistance from the company.

ASSESSMENT OF EFFECTIVENESS OF TRAINING/ EDUCATION MEASURES

Our expectations, based on a pre-visit literature search on Japanese
management education, led us to anticipate that examinations would
play an important part in any assessment of the efficacy of various
training measures. Interviewees tended to reject this suggestion and
certainly did not suggest its widespread use for middle management and
above. Moreover they suggested that where examinations did take place
they were, generally, post-promotion diagnostic tests rather than checks
or qualifying exams. However assessments were important and 'could
contain a form of examination'. Most of the larger firms tend to assess
three times a year. The spring assessment is by far the most important
and relates to promotion, career development plans and redeployment
whereas the others are more concerned with salary-related matters such
as bonuses.

    Measures to evaluate OJT, including job rotation are clearly not easy
to design. Training departments often ask for detailed reports from line
managers and supervisors on planning and completion of OJT training.
In many cases training staff will actually visit the work-place to check the
implementation of OJT (an OJT audit) and this is often checked against
a company-wide set of OJT objectives.

    Off the job training evaluation is far more systematized. The most frequently used methods of assessing the effectiveness for executives and for middle management continue to be the use of impressions of the courses by the recipients either by round table discussions, question-naires or by submission of detailed daily journals. However, there has been an almost ten per cent drop in usage of this method over the last decade or so. Conversely there has been a considerable increase in the utilization of detailed dissertations/reports with a 30 per cent increase for senior middle management and a 40 per cent increase for junior middle management. Another method with an increased usage rate is the use of in-company announcement meetings or internally circulated reports and this is very popular with top management. Hitherto the second most popular method was evaluation of actual results and activity in the place of work, but in fact this has been pushed into fourth place by these other methods. In all cases, examinations based on the contents of the courses have dropped and in no case reached even three per cent.

There is a clear trend towards the placing of more emphasis on education and training for the two top levels of management and there is now an expectation of an upsurge in training for specialists and engineers. There is now also a lower priority for new recruits.

EXTERNAL SOURCES OF MANAGEMENT TRAINING IN JAPAN

The university sector

The almost complete absence of business schools, on the Harvard model, is immediately noticeable in Japan. Only Keio Business School runs a full-time 2 year MBA programme (60 students per year) and this is not expanding. Indeed it may simply be offering a less expensive American-style MBA by keeping the students within Japan rather than drafting them overseas. So far, as a model, Keio has been a failure despite the very high quality of the course provided. Another difference is the absence of undergraduate departments of business administration and postgraduate schools in business in the national and prefectural universities. Where such departments do exist is in the private universities where an MBA-type degree can be obtained. However these MBA students usually take the MBA qualifications (in small classes) as one step on the road to teaching business studies often with a PhD to follow. Post-experience executive training of an MBA nature can be obtained at such places as the Nomura Advanced Management Centre and the Matsushita School of Government, and these are normally approved by MITI rather than the Ministry of Education. In the main, Japanese MBAs are obtained at the more prestigious overseas universities such as Harvard, MIT, London and Manchester, etc., where clearly the networking for the future and acquisition of language skills are probably more important than the subject-matter of the programmes. It is quite clear that the efforts over the last decade to develop MBA teaching in Japan, apart from in international divisions of Japanese multinationals and in foreign firms, have met with very limited success and so far there is no sign of any major expansion.

PROFESSIONAL MANAGEMENT ORGANIZATIONS

Japan's postwar management and training associations are highly professional with high-level research and teaching expertise. Essentially they are the heirs to a management revolution initiated by the Americans within Japan in the Occupation period (1945–52). American military authorities first purged many of the top managers in Japan either for being nationalists or operating the giant family combines such as Mitsui, Mitsubishi, Sumitomo, etc. They initiated the 128-hour Civil Communications Section (CCS) Management Programme and this was enthusiastically welcomed by top Japanese management. By 1952 it had spread through mining and shipbuilding. By 1952, 1287 had taken this course. The Japan Federation of Employers continued to sponsor it and then the Japan Industrial and Vocational Training Association took it over in 1955. The US Air Force also introduced the Management Training Programme (MTP) based on the work of Henri Fayol. It was originally for its 2000 supervisors at US airbases throughout Japan. It was then extended to middle management in Japan, providing the first systematized middle management training ever. The Americans recommended that MITI utilize this programme more widely, and MITI launched six courses in 1951 and then transferred responsibility for the programmes to the Japan Federation of Employers. By 1954 there were 372 instructors and the number going through the courses had reached 46 000. Another related programme was Training Within Industry (TWI) designed for supervisor training in the UK and USA during the war. Originally used to train 2000 Japanese supervisors on US Air bases in Japan the Ministry of Labour examined it in late 1948 and after about a year, having Japanized it, launched the first courses in 1950. Within one year they had over 500 trainers and almost 16 000 trainees and by end of 1952 25 000 instructors had trained 171 000 supervisors and foremen including the majority in large firms. In 1954 the Labour Ministry transferred responsibility to the Small and Medium Size Enterprise Agency and in that year the number trained reached 339 378.

The National Personnel Authority began examining MTP and TWI in 1950 and developed the NPA Supervisor Course for the public sector and the Japan Federation of Employers began using it in the private sector in 1952. By this time there were 220 trainers in the private sector alone. In 1955, the JMA and the Public Opinion Science Association took over sales of these programmes in the private sector. 1955 appears to have been a watershed year with all these American-influenced management training programmes being taken up by JIVTA, JMA, etc., and the mid-fifties also saw the so-called 'management boom' in Japan with the sales of business management books hitting record levels. Today the leading management associations are the Japan Management Association, Nippon Administrative Management Association, the Japan Productivity Association, Japan Industrial and Vocational Training Organization although they are clearly targeted at large firms. They provide not only excellent programmes but also up-to-date information on domestic and international developments as well as organizing missions overseas for Japanese managers. For example, by 1981 the Japan Productivity Centre had organized 1468 overseas missions for some 22 888 executives. Industry-wide or sectoral associations also have their own management academies offering programmes and these are often grouped into regional associations, e.g. the Junior Executive Academy of the Central Japan Industries Association.

Japan's SME sector has relied rather more heavily on industry associations, chambers of commerce and industry and specialist quasi-governmental SME organizations where the quality of courses is quite high but with the advantages of proximity and lower cost. The SME Agency has also set up the Small and Medium Size Enterprise College with 7 campuses so far throughout Japan. Especially significant are the

SME Counsellors (*Shindanshi*) now numbering over 7000 who must attend a one-year programme at this college or sit a very tough qualifying exam before practising management consultancy with small firms through the various small business associations. They, along with nearly 400 management consultant groups belonging to federations approved by MITI, provide a form off management training in the form of consultancy. Usually members of such groups must be either certified public accountants, certified tax accountants or SME Counsellors. SMEs also receive much assistance from parent or patron companies (in the case of subcontracting).

Although the government has effectively handed over the design, improvement and running of management programmes to private sector organizations, its role in setting up and continuing to support management training and development remains considerable. The Management Coordination Agency of the Government continues to monitor trends, providing more specialized data to add to that provided by the Ministry of Education (which is now developing plans for 'lifetime education'), The Prime Minister's Office, MITI, the SMEA and the Ministry of Labour plus the National Personnel Authority for the civil service. Moreover, these ministries operate various systems for vetting, approving and licensing individuals, courses and even new management organizations and schools outside the formal national education system.

PROBLEMS AHEAD

Despite the fact that Japan seems to be doing relatively well in industrial terms there are major problems appearing. At the very general level there is the reduction in employment opportunities caused by the introduction of mechatronics, office automation, etc., and the establishment of Japanese companies overseas due to export substitution measures and/or the high yen. Next there is the changing industrial structure. Japan faces two major structural shifts which impinge directly on management. The first is the continuing shift towards the tertiary sector service sector which exceeded 50 per cent for the first time in 1980. For example, the recent deregulation of the financial sector is causing traumatic changes in hiring practices with headhunting and lateral entry being carried out by even the most traditional of firms. Women are increasingly finding this sector attractive in terms of both salaries and promotion opportunities but there is a marked drop in the SME share of this sector from 85.4 per cent in 1960 to 69.2 per cent in 1981 indicating more larger firms diversifying into the area.

In 1982 the Economic Planning Agency published a document 'Japan in the Year 2000' and regarding industrial structure forecast the following (actual 1985 figures added):

Sector	1970	1980	(1985)	2000
Primary	17.4	10.4	8.8	4.9
Secondary	35.2	34.8	34.3	33.3
Tertiary	47.3	54.5	56.5	61.8
Total	100.0	100.0	100.0	100.0

Manufacturing's share of the work-force has continually declined over recent years, dropping from one-third to one-quarter as the following table shows clearly:

Year	Manuf.	Commerce	Service Industries	Construction	Mining
1963	33.3%	33.7%	13.2%	8.7%	0.7%
1966	32.2%	32.6%	13.5%	10.2%	0.6%
1969	31.7%	32.9%	13.4%	10.7%	0.5%
1972	30.3%	33.1%	13.3%	11.8%	0.4%
1975	28.3%	34.0%	13.8%	12.3	0.3%
1978	26.8%	34.6%	14.3%	12.7%	0.3%
1981	25.7%	34.9%	15.0%	12.7%	0.3%

The second structural tranformation, of an even greater traumatic potential, is the effort to transform Japan from an industrial framework designed for a 'pursuer' nation into one which will allow Japan to become a 'pioneer' nation, especially in science and technology. Already the government has been active in implementing the so-called 'SangakuKan' (Collaboration between Industry, Government and Academia) in an effort to bring universities closer to the needs of industry in research and development. A key element is creativity, and the government is utilizing this new policy to experiment with enhanced mobility of key personnel between the three sectors on secondment, etc. Central to the new industrial strategy is the targeting of the SME sector as a key area in terms of innovation, creativity, etc., in knowledge-based industries. This means that large firms will be disadvantaged, although large corporate groupings will adapt by using 'spinout' techniques to set up new subsidiaries. This has already happened in depressed industries and the management development skills of such large companies will now be offered to other companies. Kobe Steel for example has created 'Human Create' and Sumitomo Metals have launched Sumikin Intercom, essentially training companies utilizing élite trainers/educators from within their overstaffed personnel divisions.

Reduction in employment opportunities is paralleled by a major reduction in promotion openings and according to Professor Amaya 30 per cent of graduates can expect management posts in the near future, a reduction of 50 per cent. The Ministry of Labour puts the figure even lower at 20 per cent. The impact of this on morale will be considerable. In addition when management promotion does come it may well take longer to achieve. Already private research groupings are urging the government to set up counselling bodies jointly funded by industry and government for second career development, etc. Moreover, many Japanese companies are now endeavouring to develop management training opportunities which actually have as their objective preparation for future careers outside the organization in order to maintain morale. This, together with the headhunting practices appearing increasingly in the financial sector, would seem to indicate a trend towards portable qualifications. Such a trend has already been noticed by JIVTA in its national survey where it found it necessary to introduce a new category, 'company assistance with official qualifications' and between 40–50 per cent of firms of all sizes surveyed acknowledged use of this as very important. However this apparent manifestation of a 'credential society' will be in terms of government approved courses rather than MBA-type qualifications. The number of managers will be expected to drop with a subsequent increase in specialists.

MOTIVATION AND MORALE

In many respects Japan's large, internationally competitive companies are now running into trouble in terms of human resource development. Traditionally able to select the very best graduates, they are now increasingly concerned with the quality and even quantity of recruits. Many top managers we interviewed questioned whether the present generation still possessed the right attitude to work and especially work in large companies. They continually mentioned a lack of *hangarii seishin* (hungry spirit) implying that the new recruits were not so keen to work hard and devote themselves to the company. One might well say this is merely a traditional complaint of an older generation, but some Japanese see it as a direct consequence of an increasingly affluent society, the so-called 'advanced nation disease' 'British disease' or 'eurosclerosis'. Perhaps of greater significance is the fact that many of the larger firms which were able in the past to attract top graduates are suffering from two fundamental changes. The first is that the older established firms have often found themselves in depressed sectors and have had to restructure and this is manifestly less attractive to today's bright graduates. Secondly, and partly related to that, the 'sunrise' industries which are attracting young students are often small technology intensive or R & D intensive firms (venture businesses). The fact that large companies are now regarded as less attractive, old-fashioned and also incapable of offering guaranteed promotion any more, clearly is changing the nature of those being recruited. The government's policy of placing reliance on smaller-scale firms at the technological frontier is also a factor influencing today's youth.

WOMEN

By any criterion Japanese women appear less likely to enter management positions than those in any other advanced industrial country. The Prime Minister's Office gives figures of 6.7 per cent (1980) of the female workforce employed in management as compared with 23.5 per cent in USA and 39.8 in West Germany. However, this figure seems to correspond more closely to the category administration/management used by the Statistical Bureau of the Management and Coordination Agency which shows 6.6 per cent (1984) a rise of 0.6 per cent from 1982. It also fails to take into account that certain categories of clerical work may also be classified as management.Moreover, these figures are percentage of women managers in the female work-force, and perhaps the most realistic figure is the Management and Coordination Agency's figures for female managerial employees – 1960 0.3   1975 0.9   1983 0.8. (ILO also quotes 0.8 for Japan in 1982.) This reflects severe limitations on promotion of female staff, and in April this year an Equal Opportunity Law was passed to ban sexual discrimination in hiring, promotion and firing. This legislation reflects the failure of Japanese companies to adhere to constitutional stipulations on this subject and the new law promises to make management development and promotion more complex for Japanese companies. The second ranked peak business association in Japan, the Japan Committee for Economic Development (*Keizai Doyukai*) – regarded as much less conservative than the No. 1, the *Keidanren* (Japanese CBI) – has moved quickly to appoint five businesswomen as the first female members in its forty-year history. On the positive side, women are seen as more creative than their male counterparts and moreover seen as potentially able to fill the future gaps created by a rapidly ageing population and a smaller birthrate, etc. Foreign firms and increasingly the service sector – especially finance – offer by far the best opportunities for women to reach management in addition to the traditional route to management in SMEs.

AGEING WORK-FORCE

A rapidly ageing work-force is yet another problem facing the Japanese since they have a population ageing at a higher rate than any other advanced industrial nation. The erosion of the seniority-based promotion systems and pay systems continues. Retraining of workers for early retirement or secondment, redeployment to other firms in enterprise groups, to subcontractors and suppliers and to SMEs is continuing apace. Such efforts are consuming considerable time and money in terms of the training budgets although there are some government support schemes.

CONCLUSION

There is a convergence of schemes for graduate employees requiring assistance with qualifications for the future and those needed for retraining older employees. This is accompanied by an expansion of self-development programmes in which corporate training/education staff are proactive. This indicates a potential boom in second-career-type programmes especially self-development packages possibly with governmental/corporate assistance. This boom should be able to absorb demands for second-career packages for younger staff and indeed the ageing work-force as well. Japanese decision-makers, despite present successes, appear to view the future with considerable concern. Despite the fact that Japan is now a wealthy nation there seems little danger of complacency emerging. Problems within Japan as well as threats from tariff barriers, newly industrializing countries, etc., ensure that Japan's policymakers continue to plan ahead in order to maintain or even enhance Japan's position as a world leader. The Japanese data on existing management education and development practices is superb and they are well aware of the need to strive for continuous improvement. One must assume that a nation which places such great and continuing efforts into devising, developing and monitoring human resource development practices, is very well equipped to adapt to the needs of the 1990s and beyond. Nevertheless Japan's comparative advantage hitherto has lain with its manufacturing sector and we should still look to this sector for lessons to be learned. However, in the services sector, now expanding rapidly, really effective Japanese management development practices have not yet evolved. It may well be that they must again learn from us in this area where we may still possess some advantage. However, we can only hope to match Japanese achievements if we are prepared to work at it as hard and as systematically as our Japanese competitors. In terms of management education, there are no secrets, no array of techniques unknown in the West. Most Japanese methods and techniques originated in the West. The Japanese have modified and refined these somewhat. However it is the consistent, systematic and integrated application of these techniques, allied with management's lifelong interest in learning, and especially learning from others, which has helped Japan develop a professional management cadre capable of keeping them competitive in the years to come.

3 THE UNITED STATES

BY CHARLES HANDY

It is the numbers which make the first impression on any visitor to the United States. Even when all numbers are divided by four to make them comparable with Britain they are still huge. Americans do most things on a large scale and, to some extent, quantity compensates for any loss of quality. Management education and training is no exception. Nell Eurich estimates that American corporations alone may spend some $60 billion on training their employees of which perhaps $13 billion goes to management training[1].

The second impression is that the frontier mentality is still alive and thriving in America. Although the self-confidence has been dented recently, there is still the belief that the golden age lies in the future not the past, that almost anything is possible and, above all, that every individual has the chance to influence his or her destiny, that there is room for all to succeed and that nothing has been predetermined at birth. Any limits to self-improvement are ultimately self-imposed.

From this stems, probably, the prevailing sense of the market-place. Society is widely perceived as a market-place for talent, as well as for goods and services. If you have something good to offer there is likely to be someone somewhere who will want to buy it. It is a big market-place, one which will often involve travelling or changing homes but there is a remarkable homogeneity and a lack of regional tribalism which makes mobility less painful.

Not unnaturally, therefore, most Americans are intuitively aware of business realities. One chief executive said that 'every American, male and female, grows up thinking of themselves as being in business whatever it is that they end up doing as a career'. The manager or businessman in America is not only widely accepted but can attain the position of folk-heroes, as with Iaccoca of Chrysler in recent years.

In 1983, in one survey, 55 per cent of male college freshmen, for instance, and, even more significantly 43 per cent of females said that 'being successful in a business of my own' was either essential or very important[2].

Given this tradition it is natural that education should be seen as an important investment. It is one obvious way to improve your chances and to gain credentials in the market-place. American universities were not slow to recognize the importance of professional education in all sectors with the result that the preparation for the professions started in the universities, not in the professions as in Europe. At the turn of the century business schools were added to the growing list of other professional schools with a teaching method originally based on that of the university law schools.

It is therefore formal education which forms the backbone of America's approach to the development of her managers. There is *individual education*, undertaken by the individual before entry or soon after entry and there is *corporate education*, education sponsored or managed by the corporations. Both of these assume some definition of the job of the manager and of the key elements of an effective business. This definition has recently begun to be modified and this in turn is having its repercussions in the corporate classrooms of America and, to a lesser extent, in its business schools.

No discussion of management education and development in America would, however, be complete without some overview of the general educational infrastructure from which all managers originate and of the way their careers and lives have traditionally progressed.

THE EDUCATIONAL INFRASTRUCTURE

The Americans favour a broad general education extending on into the early college or university years. Specialization comes late and flowers in the variety of graduate schools for every profession or vocation.

Most Americans attend a local high school, either from 12–17 years or 14–17 years. In the majority of states, education is compulsory up to 16 and in a few until 17. Eleven per cent (a percentage higher, actually, than in Britain) attend private schools at the same ages[2].

Seventy-two per cent of 18-year-olds have a High School Diploma. These diplomas require a specified minimum number of course credits, some in subjects laid down by the state. Most states also require proficiency tests in particular areas. There is not therefore any agreed national curriculum or national standards. In 1982, in fact, 88 per cent of all high school seniors described their studies as an 'academic programme'; 36 per cent described them as a 'general programme' while 27 per cent called them 'vocational'.

There is considerable disquiet in America about the quality of much of the education, with surveys and stories of large groups of university students unable to identify America on a map of the world or unable to spell simple words. 'A Nation at Risk', the report of the National Commission on Excellence in Education, published in 1983, focused national attention on educational reform.

Nonetheless, the USA educates more people for longer than anyone else except Japan. Almost half of those graduating with a high school diploma will go on to study in college, either a four-year undergraduate college or a two-year community college awarding an associate degree. These community colleges, mostly part-time and open entry, are accounting for an increasing proportion of higher education in the USA. It is estimated, as a result, that by 1992 nearly 50 per cent of students in higher education will be over 25 years of age and that 46 per cent will be studying part-time.

However, in spite of the growth of the part-timers 86 per cent of undergraduate degrees are still today in full-time four-year colleges and 22 per cent of an age group will be studying there (compared with 14 per cent in Britain). In general, two of the four years will be a mixed blend of subjects with only the final two geared to a speciality or 'major'. In 1986 nearly 24 per cent of these 'majors' were in business and management. There were, therefore, 240 000 students graduating in business-related studies, in 1986. If all these entered some form of managerial career it would mean that something like two-thirds of all America's new managers would have studied the subject at undergraduate school.

Americans, as we have already noted, do not think that education finishes at 18. In October 1982 there were 18.2 million people enrolled in some programme beyond secondary level: 9.2 million were studying for a degree, 3.8 million for a vocational certificate and 5.2 million for personal development or interest, without credit. These numbers are huge, even allowing for the fact that America is four times larger in population than Britain or France or Germany. Whatever the doubts about some of the quality there can be no question about the quantity of education in America at all ages.

Education plays a big part in American life. Teachers and professors are respected. Degrees and qualifications are desired and sought after. It is a natural and normal instinct in America to want to go back to school throughout life. Faced with new problems or new opportunities Americans often turn first to the universities and colleges for help through research, teaching or consultancy.

It was, therefore, quite natural for education to embrace business and management. The first business schools and the first degrees in business occurred at the beginning of the century. To an American there has never been anything unusual about going to school to learn about business and management. In this Americans have been different from other societies. The difference has its roots in the American culture of self-improvement and in the pervasive educational infrastructure which leaves few untouched.

THE MANAGER IN AMERICA

The word 'manager' has no formal or legal definition in America. It is used interchangeably with 'executive' or 'administrator'. No one knows how many managers there are. 11.5 million people (11.5 per cent of the work-force) in the 1980 census described themselves as managers or administrators but this figure is widely thought to exaggerate the true position.

The word 'manager' is used to describe very different kinds of people. Schein[4] identified six different managerial roles:

- The specialist contributor
- The project manager
- The functional manager
- The general manager
- The entrepreneur
- The consultant.

All can be called, interchangeably, manager or executive. The term 'manager' is often as much to do with status as with function, the first-line supervisor in many large companies being called manager in order to increase the sense of identification with the companies' goals and philosophy. The word 'executive' is widely used to describe anyone with budget responsibilities.

The significance of this is important. It means that business and management education is deemed to be appropriate to a very wide range of people. There is no feeling now in America of a managerial cadre, of people who do the managing whilst others do the operations.

The corporate manager has always been regarded in America as a serious and important role, well remunerated, well regarded and well documented in literature and in surveys. One of the more recent of such surveys was one carried out by Korn Ferry International in conjunction with the UCLA Graduate School of Management[5]. It was a survey of 4350 vice-presidents and corporate specialists in the top 1000 companies. The survey presents the following composite picture of the senior American manager or executive to-day (excerpts):

'Our composite executive sees integrity as the most important element in a successful business career, concern for results and a desire for responsibility are also deemed necessary. He does not attribute much importance to likeability and appearance, or, surprisingly, to formal business training. However, he does feel that *general* education can have a significant impact on career development'.

'In his own personal advancement, he firmly believes that hard work was the single most important factor in bringing about his success. Ambition and luck also figured prominently. Although our executive is currently in general management he began his career in finance/accounting. Most of his peers are also in general management but they too started out in a different functional area. He has worked for two companies in his career and now earns $215 000 plus fringe benefits and options.'

By comparison with a similar 1979 survey the 1986 executive is two years younger, better paid in real terms, takes fewer vacations and is more ambitious, but has a similar educational and social background.

Statistically, 85 per cent of the respondents had a college degree (51 per cent Bachelor of Science and 49 per cent Bachelor of Arts). More than half (51 per cent) of the respondents had a graduate degree of which the MBA accounted for 54 per cent with Law in second place at 22 per cent. Fifty-six per cent first earned money outside the home between the ages of 11 and 15 and a further 30 per cent before they were 20.

Current evidence suggests that in 20 years' time a similar sample will be younger, more female, even more formally qualified, will have changed companies more often and may be more interested in running its own businesses than in reaching the top of the corporate ladder.

The survey confirms the cultural stereotype. Successful American managers start earning money as teenagers, business is in their blood. They pay some of their own way through college by working while they study – making education into a very personal investment. A university degree seems almost a necessary starting condition, increasingly followed by a graduate degree, usually in business. But it is education not training which they value, and particularly education with a formal qualification at the end of it. They work hard and earn well, but are prepared to move to find the opportunities they want. In short, education, hard work and a market-place for their talents seems to be the recipe for the management development of today's senior managers. It is a very American way.

INDIVIDUAL EDUCATION

A business 'major' is now by far the most popular undergraduate degree and an MBA by far the most popular graduate or professional qualification, with 240 000 BBAs and 70 000 MBAs graduating in 1987 (almost one quarter of the total in each case).

This is a relatively recent phenomenon. In 1960 less than 5000 MBAs were granted. There is however no standardization of the product. 'Business and Management' covers a wide diversity of undergraduate degrees with 14 383 majoring in 'banking and finance' in 1981–2 and 26 945 in 'marketing and purchasing'. Similarly the MBA label covers many brands. No one knows how many MBA programmes there are, but some estimates run as high as 1000. Only 204 of these had recognition and accreditation in 1984 from the AACSB (the acrediting body for business education). The great majority of these degrees are for one year or the part-time equivalent of one year and are more truly the fifth or specialist year added on to a four-year undergraduate course. Such degrees do not bear comparison with the intensive programmes at the famous business schools yet they are all lumped together as MBAs.

As one result, the MBA degree encounters a lot of cynicism from employers, some of whom have called it the most oversold degree in history. That does not stop ever greater numbers of young men, and, increasingly, young women, from studying for it, whether it is officially accredited or not, seemingly on the grounds that some educational clothing is better than none at all in an increasingly competitive market for talent and in an occupation where a level of formal knowledge and analytical skills is assumed.

A second result of the variety of MBA degrees is a clear institutional pecking order. *Where* you get your MBA is critical to an assessment of its worth and your work. The Top Ten are dominated by the prestigious private institutions such as Harvard, Stanford, Wharton and Chicago, who offer two-year MBAs but do not, normally, offer undergraduate degrees (Wharton is the exception). There are a further 20 or so two-year programmes in well-known universities, many of them state universities, and then there are the rest, some of them huge like Pace University in New York State which can graduate up to 8000 MBAs in a year (more than five times the current total for the whole of the UK). Some are well known for a particular speciality (e.g. International Studies at Thunderbird) and some are known for nothing particular at all but thrive on their affiliation with local business from which they draw their hundreds and even thousands of part-time students and many part-time teachers.

The 'local' universities and colleges thrive on the tradition of tuition reimbursement in American corporations, whereby the company reimburses individuals for all or part of their study costs if the course is considered relevant to their careers. The tuition reimbursement is seen as almost akin to an individual right, part of the conditions of service, and can lead to the apparently contradictory situation in which the corporation sees little direct value to itself in the course but would still allow the individual to do it. It is a part of that American tradition which holds that education is an individual's way of improving his or her chances in life, an investment made largely by the individual and at the individual's discretion. It is this tradition which explains the continual explosion of BBA and MBA degrees (see Table 3.1) in spite of considerable criticism of the courses by many employers. In spite of this criticism, those selfsame employers will often be found stalking the best students at the top schools (Goldman Sachs alone recruited 44 members of the 1986 Harvard Class).

The attitude seems to be that as long as the MBA is regarded by young people as an indispensable asset then the schools become the obvious recruiting grounds for talent, irrespective of what students have learnt while they are there. The schools themselves, therefore, confronted by queues of eager applicants *and* of recruiters from the best companies see no immediate need to change what they do. The signals from the market-place appear to indicate that the product is all right.

Table 3.1: Masters' and Bachelors' degrees gained in US business and management 1963/4 to 1983/4

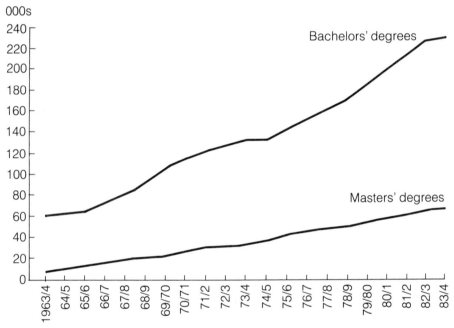

Source: US Department of Education, Centre for Education Statistics, 'Earned degrees conferred' surveys, July 1986

The criticisms, however, are serious. The business schools are attacked by some for:

(a) ignoring some of the more important aspects of management, human skills, entrepreneurship and internationalism, in favour of the easier to teach analytical skills of finance and marketing;

(b) fostering undesirable attitudes – short-run thinking and unrealistic job expectations.

Others believe that the schools have abandoned the search for fresh intellectual foundations, preferring to codify and interpret current practice, and that they are, for example, neglecting the traditions and disciplines of history, political theory, philosophy and ethics, scientific method and creative literature which are more than ever needed by the international manager moving in new and complex worlds.

A further strand of criticism focuses on the growing popularity of undergraduate business studies, and questions the need for a long *general* instruction to business and management at the graduate level if more and more people have already done it as undergraduates, (50 per cent of MBAs are already business majors). The MBA of the future, these people argue should be a shorter, more specialist programme taken after a first degree in business and after some relevant experience, often part-time. Some go on to argue the need for an Executive *Doctor* of Business Administration (DBA) for high-level specialists and consultants who want to keep at the leading edge of their field.

These arguments and criticisms are, however, about methods and curricula. They do not alter or attempt to deny a widely held assumption in the USA, that a general grounding in the language and methods of business is a useful, if not essential, preliminary to any career in business or management and, that it is primarily, an *individual's* responsibility to acquire this grounding, although benevolent corporations should do what they can to help.

Many Americans, however, are beginning to worry that this business literacy is acquired at some cost, that such vocationalism leaves less room for exploration of other subjects, for the skills of communication, for wider reading and wider enquiry. 'They know everything about business and nothing about anything else.' 'They are the best educated and the worst educated at the same time.' A businesslike but narrow-minded USA is their fear for the future, a future, they believe, in which breadth of vision and the capacity to learn anew will be more important than any analytical skills.

It is, perhaps, an American paradox that the very strength of their educational tradition seems to make it almost immune to criticism. Americans in business are educated, of that the statistics leave one in no doubt, but if they are wrongly educated, it may turn out to be a danger not a help. It is this underlying worry which is causing more and more corporations to take corporate education much more seriously than ever before.

CORPORATE EDUCATION

Education is big business in America's larger corporations. Dr Nell Eurich's estimate of perhaps $60 billion a year in total spent on education and training is so large a number that it is almost meaningless, but of this she believes that $13 billion will have been spent on management education and training and of this amount again $600 million will have gone to graduate schools of business administration for their executive programmes[1].

A.T. and T. before divestiture in 1984 had one million employees and reportedly spent $1.7 billion on employee training in 1980 and perhaps $2 billion in 1982. They conducted 12 000 courses in 1300 locations for 20 000–30 000 employees *per day* with 13 000 trainees and support staff. One analysis concluded that A.T. and T. performed more education and training than any university in the world. There is no reason to believe that the separate parts of the company now, several years later, spend any less money or time.

Companies such as Xerox and IBM reckon to spend about 1.6 per cent of *turnover* on training of all types or about $2000 per employee per year, excluding the wages and salaries of the trainees – an annual total of $200 million for Xerox and $800 million for IBM. If the time of the trainees is costed and included the figure rises to $2 billion.

That last figure compares with IBM's expenditure on R & D of some $3 billion a year.

A.T. and T. as it was, IBM and Xerox are some of the more conspicuous spenders, but their example is followed by most of the top 1000 corporations in America. Many of them have their own private campuses or 'corporate colleges' such as the Holiday Inn University, Dana University, Xerox's Learning Center in Leasburg Virginia with up to 14 000 students per year. Western Electric's Corporate Education Center in Princeton is typical: 300 acres of landscaped grounds, spacious private rooms with baths, excellent kitchens and good sports facilities. Cocooned in comfort, the executives have little to distract them from serious discussion, debate and learning.

Education, however, is not confined to these exotic settings. It usually reaches out into all the many bits of the business in many different guises. A corporation will buy courses from consultants, will contract with a college or a university for tailor-made programmes, will design its own courses with outside input, will send chosen individuals away to executive programs and provide tuition reimbursement schemes for self-initiated studies.

The education, moreover, is of all sorts. There are remedial programmes, covering topics such as effective writing that should have been mastered in school or colleges; there is technical and scientific education ranging from high-school level to post-doctoral study. General Electric's basic engineering course (three years long) called the ABC, began in 1923 and now has participants from other companies while Wang, Rand and Arthur D. Little offer MSc degrees. There is education in the humanities, such as Kimberly-Clark's course on 'Image of Business in Literature' and, of course, most commonly there is education for practising management. Management education programmes typically include elements on managing *people*, managing *money*, managing *operations* and, in the senior levels, managing *the future* (or corporate strategy).

Twenty-five years ago Professor Jay Forester suggested that managers ought to be spending twenty-five per cent of their time developing themselves for the future[6]. American corporations do not carry it that far yet, but 42 per cent of the top 300 companies expect to give their managers at least five days off-the-job education every year. Some, like IBM, guarantee it. Some exceed the five days by a factor of two or even three. Education, in these companies, is thought to be good for the individual and for the company. (See Table 3.2.)

External programmes

10 000 executives enrolled in 1981 on the programmes taught at the 150 business schools offering executive education. It is a far cry from the 360 executives in 1945 who enrolled in the first programmes offered to

Table 3.2: Executives' time in training in the USA

(% of participating companies in which executives spend more than five days/year in training)

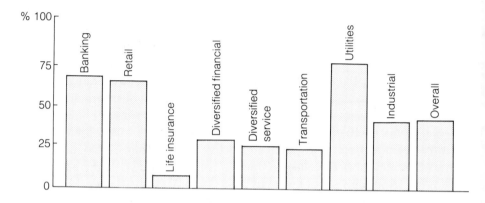

Source: Survey of top 300 companies by Executive Knowledgeworks, 1986

executives, at Harvard. It will be many more than 10 000 by the end of the 1980s[7].

Already, in 1981, over 86 per cent of 300 top companies were sponsoring candidates on campus-based programmes of at least two weeks in length. Another survey, in 1986, of 300 top corporations confirmed these sort of figures. (See Table 3.3.)

The external programmes are largely seen as compressed business education, updating the knowledge and skills of people already holding an MBA or compensating, a little, for the lack of that early formal grounding.

The Executive MBA (EMBA) is an explicit overlap between corporate education and individual education. The Executive MBAs are part-time courses for executives, usually in their mid-thirties to mid-forties, often conducted on alternate Fridays and Saturdays, occasionally in the evenings. In 1974 there were 10 schools offering such programmes, now there are 100. The tuition costs are usually borne by the company. Some programmes are geared to specific industries (e.g. information technology) and there are now discussions in process about creating Executive MBAs for specific corporations, although most of the business schools see dangers in such a tight linkage. It would threaten, they believe, the objectivity which is a large part of the value of an external programme as well as the interchange with another set of managers.

Table 3.3: Use of university programmes

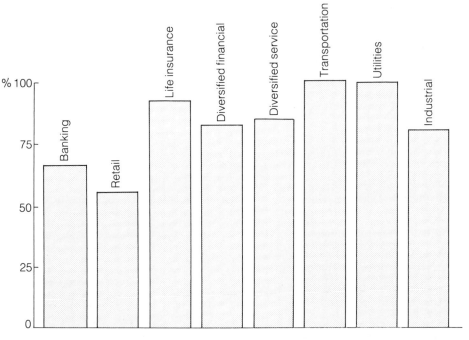

Source: Executive Knowledgeworks, 1986

There are also some doubts expressed about the quality of some EMBA programmes. It is, perhaps, harder to be rigorous when all the participants are employed by the same company and where failure, therefore, would be conspicuous.

The Executive MBA, however, is the natural outcome of a system and a culture which puts a high value on formal education and on its hallmarks (the degrees). Americans, like most people, would prefer to be paid and to be working while they study, but that study should result in a personal credential for them. The Executive MBA and tuition reimbursement is one American response. The tradition goes wider than MBA, of course. One estimate is that within adult education as a whole, corporations paid for over 12 million courses while individuals and their families paid for 17 million[1].

What are people studying and why? Most of these courses are job-related, with business pre-eminent (8½ million courses taken) with health care and health sciences (nearly 4 million courses) and engineering and technology ($3\frac{1}{2}$ million) following behind.

The result of corporation support for education is an increasingly well-educated work-force. Those who do not get the relevant education before they start their careers are not short of the opportunities to catch up. Those who need up-dating or to change direction have, in most large corporations, only to ask. It is, in the favoured phrase, a case of 'individual initiative and corporate support'.

Internal programmes

External programmes can, however, be only a partial answer to corporate education. For one thing, there are never going to be enough of them to educate the whole of a managerial stratum. 10 000 students a year may be a lot of students but it does not begin to make a dent in the numbers of middle-managers in America's corporations. For another, the corporation has too little control or influence over the programme, be it a two-week executive seminar or a two-year EMBA.

Corporate education, therefore, has increasingly taken place inside the corporation, planned, directed and initiated by the corporation for the people whom the corporation thinks would benefit from it. In this respect American corporations are no different from large corporations everywhere.

They differ from other nationalities in the way they seek, even within the corporation, to keep the university and educational flavour. What other countries would call a training centre the Americans prefer to describe as a 'learning center', a corporate 'university', an institute or a college. These 'corporate campuses' have their 'faculties' and 'associate faculties', often drawn from business schools on a part-time basis. It is 'executive education' rather than 'management training' which they offer (and two thirds of the top 300 companies have a formal executive education programme). Typically, and in line with big companies elsewhere, certain programmes are tailored to career stages, with every high potential manager expected to go on an Advanced Management Programme or its equivalent in mid-career. Such programmes do not differ markedly from those on offer in the business schools except for the fact that they are focused on one industry and one company.In 1984 Samuel A. Pond concluded that the amount of executive education conducted by the universities *inside* corporations exceeded that which they did on their own campuses.

The corporate campus is the outward and visible sign of a massive commitment to education by some of America's big corporations. The case studies at the end of this chapter give some flavour of their approach, typified perhaps by the statement from the president of Boeing Aerospace that 'in this dynamic, competitive environment, the importance of keeping your skills, knowledge and effort current is critical for the company', or that from the president of IBM that 'education is an IBM tradition. Every chairman of IBM has recognized the critical importance of helping people develop themselves to their full potential'.

There are caveats to all this activity. Many of the courses are of the 'dog and pony show' variety, exposing managers to a visiting circus of lecturers without a very well thought-through strategy or theory of learning. There is not always a deliberate attempt to monitor the annual hours spent by each individual in education even by those companies who claim to have such a policy. Human skills are not easily learnt in a classroom, although all programmes purport to teach them. The programmes may be concentrating on the wrong things, or on yesterday's problems. Some see the executive education world as a thriving self-sustaining industry, with its 250 000 full-time trainers and 500 000 part-timers[1], offering collusive partnerships between programme providers outside the organization and programme purchasers inside with no obvious way of checking on long-term results.

Indeed, one survey by Executive Knowledgeworkers[8] found that as spending on executive education increased across their sample of top companies, sales or assets per employee *decreased* (except in retail). One explanation is that declining companies need more education than fast-growing ones and have the foresightedness to spend more when they can least afford it. A more cynical explanation is that corporate education is more to do with fashion and ritual than with effectiveness. Big corporations have executive education programmes almost as a symbol of their success.

That last comment is probably too cynical by far, although some believe that very little executive education or training goes on outside the top 1000 corporations, all employing more than 10 000 people. However, a 1986 telephone survey[9] of a randomized sample of 764 companies, all with more than 250 employees, found that 80 per cent earmarked money for training each year and in these companies overall the trainees estimated that on average 38 per cent of the total work-force participated in some form of training in 1985.

The trend, however, is towards even more emphasis on the reality of the business and less on general education. Another survey[7] found that the chief executive officers were getting more personally involved, with customized courses and more problem-based seminars for chosen managers. Reality is, perhaps, driving out ritual in corporate America.

General development

In spite of all the razzmatazz of the corporate classroom and executive development programmes, most personnel officers agree that formal classroom learning by itself accounts for only 10–20 per cent of all personal learning in management. To be fully effective, any classroom learning needs to be part of a bigger process of development and to be linked into a plan and a pattern of job and career development.

This is beginning to happen more widely. The front-runners such as IBM, Boeing, General Motors, Hewlett-Packard and others have been doing it for years, as have big companies around the world. In too many others, however, education has been on a 'nice-to-know' basis and training on the 'train and hope' philosophy, in spite of a well-established train of research findings that information learnt in a vaccuum tends to evaporate very quickly. A recent survey by the Conference Board in New York[10] is therefore consoling. Three out of every five companies surveyed reported a greater use of job-descriptions and performance appraisals to identify training needs, particularly for individuals of high potential. They also report that training managers in these companies are working more closely with senior managers to help them to interpret the training implications of the new technologies and the new operating systems and to judge the role of training in improving unit performance. The questions are revealing:

'Management has become convinced that education drives the business'.

'A step-child until recently, the training function is now seen as essential to the company's strategic goods'.

'Our human resources function was given a new charter three years ago – to contribute to the company's competitive edge by recruiting talented people, training them and letting them not stagnate'.

The quotations are revealing, coming as they do from the personnel function, in that they suggest that the new infusion of reality is so recent.

When education and training have to be related to the needs of the business and to be tied to unit performance new priorities start to emerge. For top management the priorities are questions of strategic direction, of leadership and of the world outside the corporation, for middle managers the priority often is one of group performance, of interaction with their immediate colleagues. These priorities can only be addressed by the actual working groups learning together. Thus it is that the new pattern emerges of intense two or three-day seminars for particular groups of managers with a clear focus and definite expectations of some concrete result. Individual, long-term education may still be thought to be necessary but it is certainly not sufficient. The new books on management which now reach best-seller lists are all concerned with the softer skills of leadership, communication, strategy and change. The new realization is that these softer skills cannot be properly learnt in isolation.

Focused education gets a new thrust from the flattening-out and the 'downsizing' of organizations. Faced with increasing competition, American companies can no longer afford to have layers of supervisors supervising each other, of specialists and staff officers advising and checking. General Electric reduced its 400 000 staff by 100 000 over three years and saw its turnover increase as well as its profit. The 100 000 were not shop-floor workers but mostly staffers or, as it turned out, 'extras'. Fewer levels of command and fewer specialist roles mean more responsibilities devoted to the operational unit along with more joint problem-solving by cross-functional teams. This only works if the competence of those working at this level is increased and if there is a deliberate 'upskilling' in the softer skills for all managers and workers. One consequence therefore, of the restructuring of much of American business has been a change in the focus of its training and a new sense of urgency in its delivery.

This shift in emphasis is not confined to the large and famous corporations. Indeed it is some of the newer and smaller organizations which are often leading the way; organizations such as Worthington Industries, Stew Leonard's and W.L. Gore have been identified by Tom

Peters[11] as leading the new wave of management in America, one in which education and training is seen as a continuing and vital ingredient in effectiveness.

In these newer businesses, change is a constant companion, responsibility comes early and career development is more a sequence of opposition than a planned journey up a ladder. Apple Computers, for instance, has no pension plan because it expects its 30-year-old managers to move on within ten years at most, having gained valuable experience, backed up by the training programmes available at Apple University.

A venture capital banker insists that the managers of any of the new ventures which he finances must have previously had overall operating responsibility and he now finds many in their late twenties or early thirties who can meet this requirement, often having changed companies in order to get the experience they needed. It is this sense of an open market for talent which has persuaded most of America's smaller companies that it is unnecessary for them to invest in career development plans or orchestrated executive education programmes.

'We expect them to be competent when they arrive' one chief executive said, and another 'We believe that a good manager will learn from his own experience and will find out what he needs to know from his colleagues'.

That may be wishful thinking, but it encapsulates the feeling among the smaller businesses that experience is the only school worth having. The more progressive new companies build on this feeling by creating a culture where mistakes are accepted and forgiven provided one learns from them, where the learning from one's colleagues is encouraged by group seminars and specially-designed study modules, and where the group is encouraged to think of itself as a learning network in which it is acceptable to ask for help and to admit ignorance.

A COMMENTARY

The strength of American management starts with an infrastructure of an early education in business. It can be assumed today that almost every aspiring manager in America's big companies is a graduate in some discipline and will in some way have studied the language and methods of business before he or she is 35. People may dispute the quality of much of this education but no one can dispute the quantity. American executives are educated.

This early experience of education reinforces a respect and a desire for learning and for self-development, which is part of the national culture. Many a bookshop in America will have its display of business books right near the entrance, not tucked away at the back among the special interest topics, but they will nearly all be books of the 'how to succeed variety'. This learning culture is built on by the biggest and the best firms, some in very obvious and very systematic ways, some more subtly, some both.

In general, the philosophy of the organizations is that the individual is responsible for his or her own development with, in the most cases, the active support and encouragement of the organization. The big corporations like to grow their own managers, partly because it is cheaper, partly because it encourages a sense of identity and community, but few will today actually guarantee lifetime careers. The smaller organizations do not even pretend to. They shop for talent in the market-place, often riding on the back of their bigger brothers, using them as the schools and the proving grounds for their future managers. This does not seem to be actively resented by the larger corporations who see it partly as a fact of life, partly as a way of getting their friends into positions of influence among their customers and their suppliers and, positively, as a challenge to themselves to retain the best.

Some people, as we have noted, suggest that a lot of corporate education in the past has been ritual, even damaging ritual, with a week's course on human relations substituting for proper coaching on the job. 'Courses here', at one corporate institute, 'were intellectual holiday camps – executive perks'. Where this was true it seems to be changing as more and more chief executives realize that education at all levels is a strategic importance and also that it cannot be effective in a vacuum.

Most commentators therefore expect to see a major change in the practices of management education in America. General education, including a general business education, will remain the individual's responsibility and will increasingly be a standard requirement of employment in any major corporation. It may not always be good but you will be expected to have done it and the best schools will still attract the best students even if they teach them the wrong things (in the eyes of some employers). There may, however, be more specialist MBAs developed, built on a base of undergraduate studies and fitting the individual for immediate work.

Corporate education will be increasingly in-house and will be more and more tailored to the issues of the moment, to particular work groups and their problems, and to the softer skills of leadership and group working. Several organizations, for example, have designed corporation-wide programmes on 'quality' in recent years, seeking to change a corporate culture by a mixture of new priorities, new systems and a sequence of group training programmes. Others will base a top-management programme around an analysis of competitor strengths and weaknesses in an attempt to work at a coherent and agreed strategy. Not all of these activities will necessarily be labelled 'education' or 'training' but that is what they will be, and there is likely to be a lot of these sort of initiatives in small as well as big companies, partly because they do not necessarily require a corporate campus or a permanent 'faculty'.

The idea that the leadership of a company should be involved in an almost continuous seminar, backed up by extensive reading, consultations with experts, periods of reflection, and an array of situation analyses is becoming more widely talked about. Forester's idea of 25 per cent of time allocated to self-development begins to make sense when it is seen as a *corporate* learning activity.

More people are going to have business and management responsibilities as part of their specialist roles. A flattening of the structure will create more smaller business units and will force the specialists within these units to play a bigger role in their decisions and their management. They will want to educate themselves for these responsibilities. At the same time, promotional opportunities will be fewer within the corporation because the ladders will be shorter. More people will look for opportunities outside. There will also be more competition. Women are expected to account for half of all business degrees by the mid-1990s. They are not going readily to settle for housework after that form of personal investment. At the same time there will be a growing shortage of semi-skilled jobs forcing more young people to get qualified skills if they want work.

All of these pressures will increase the demand for education as people seek to increase their personal worth in the market-place for talent. Demographic changes notwithstanding, therefore, we can expect to see more and more MBAs in America, often of a part-time nature, and more and more internal and focused learning within companies. It will be more, but it will be different, and it will continue right to the top of the organization.

It is one more paradox. Many believe that management education has, to some extent failed America, that the business schools are investigating yesterday's problems and teaching irrelevant skills, while corporate education has been more for show than for effectiveness. The trade deficit, they argue, is evidence of America's falling competitiveness and managerial weakness. The reaction, however, is not to turn their backs on education but to do even more of it and to ask more of it. It is, on the face of it, an entirely healthy reaction if it works but, then, management education, like so much else in America, is a vast non-system, unco-ordinated, undirected, unplanned. No result can be guaranteed.

Parts of that non-system are impressive, magnificent even. Parts are chaos. No one can describe it adequately. It rests, however, on the underlying belief, stated at the beginning of this chapter, that every individual is ultimately responsible for his or her own destiny and that education is one way to shape that destiny. That belief is unlikely to change. It puts a big responsibility on those who are in charge of education, in the schools, the universities and the corporations, to see that their education measures up to the expectations of it. It is encouraging to see that so many are rethinking their assumptions.

It was Akio Morita, Chairman of Sony, who said 'The problem in the United States is management. Instead of meeting the challenge of a changing world, American business today is making small, short-term adjustments by cutting costs, by turning to the government for temporary relief. Success in trade is the result of patience and meticulous preparations'[12]. Part of those preparations is the education of a new generation of managers.

THE CASE STUDIES

Statistics and generalities are poor ways to convey a flavour of the educational effort in American business. The case studies show what those statistics mean in practice in one large university and in three of America's largest corporations.

16 December 1987

Management Education, Training and Development in The Boeing Company

1   The Boeing Company employs approximately 126 000 people: 89 000 of these are employed within 30 minutes travel time (car) from Seattle. Annual sales are $16 billion. The production lines in the Seattle area are very impressive with, at the time of the study, a 737 aircraft being produced every 36 hours.

2   There is strong commitment from top and senior management in Boeing to management training and development. For example, in Boeing Aerospace the president said recently, in a message to all employees, that Boeing offered 'numerous education and training programmes', and that 'the development of each manager should be a planned, continuous process that effectively satisfies both the needs of the company and the development needs of individual managers'.

3   The president of Boeing Commercial Airplane Company (one of the major operating divisions) recently said, 'as managers we are experiencing a changing environment that requires each of us to learn different management skills and to sharpen our existing skills'. He also said that the company will 'provide a clear and common sense of direction for management development with the objective of improving the effectiveness of each manager. . .'. The objectives of the company are described as 'the establishment of a planned, continuous management development process that effectively satisfies both the needs of the company and the needs of managers through the assessment and satisfaction of each manager's development requirements'.

5   Much of today's policy saw its origin in a 1977 Statement on Management Development. Key elements in today's policy include the following:

Pre-management programme
This programme consists of a three-hour seminar once a week for 14 weeks. It is designed to give a general understanding of basic management principles and objectives; to assist people to decide whether they have the interest and potential to become a Boeing supervisor; and to provide a pool of employees who have an understanding of basic

management principles (for possible future placement in supervision).

First line supervision
This is a 40-hour course for newly-appointed front-line supervisors and covers Motivation, Effective Communications, Employee Development, Marketing Leadership, Health and Safety, Equal Employment Opportunity, Personnel Practices, Resource Utilization, Delegation and Problem Solving. (It should be noted that all first-line supervisors are designated 'managers'.)

Management for Excellence seminar
The 'Management for Excellence' seminar is mainly designed for helping middle managers improve their problem-solving, decision-making and action-taking capabilities. The seminars run for five consecutive days, and managers are mixed by function and organization.

Senior management seminar
This seminar lasts two weeks and is run for managers with at least two levels of subordinate managers. The objectives are: to review the fundamentals of professional management; to provide an understanding of the Boeing Company as a corporation; and to encourage and guide planning for the future on the part of each participant. This course is considered to be a key element in nurturing managerial talent, and especially to begin the development of a generalist outlook.

Manufacturing seminar
Once a year the University of Washington Graduate School of Business Administration conducts a Manufacturing Seminar, which runs for 15 days. The objectives are to improve the professional effectiveness of Boeing managers in manufacturing, and managers in engineering, finance, materials, who have a close liaison with the manufacturing function.

University executive programme
These external programmes range from 4 to 14 weeks, and are designed for middle managers being considered for more senior level positions 'who can benefit from the revitalizing effects of exposure to new ideas, association with managers from other businesses, and the perspective

that time spent in a university environment can give'.

Sloan Fellowship
Boeing also participates in Stanford University and MIT Sloan Fellowship programmes, in order to give a few select candidates with high potential for future executive assignments an opportunity to receive an extensive industrial management education. Four-fifths of the top 30 executives in the company have been on the Sloan programme.

6   In addition to these management development programmes a very wide range of 'on hours' and 'off hours' courses are provided by the Boeing operating organizations; these cater for all the 'technical' aspects of management and marketing, and broader management topics. Each member company has a Learning Centre whereby managers (and other staff as well) can avail themselves of independent study courses using advanced learning techniques.

7   Through in-house programmes engineers can keep abreast of latest technological developments, and (at Boeing Aerospace) facilities are offered in-house for employees to obtain advanced degrees through televised classes via the University of Washington.

8   Boeing has recently joined the 'National Technological University', a consortium of more than 20 universities which link engineers and managers to degree programmes through satellite transmissions.

9   Boeing is a 'learning company' in the fullest sense. There is much more than a formal commitment to education, training and development. The president of Boeing Aerospace Company says that 'Boeing Aerospace Company's success is clearly linked to people who keep abreast of the latest technology', and that it is his hope that employees 'would take advantage of these tremendous opportunities – both for personal growth and to help Boeing Aerospace Company maintain its position on the cutting edge of technology'. It is clear that his sentiments are reflected in company policy and practice. A training manager said there is in fact 'a very high level of top management commitment'. One example is that ten vice-presidents in the Boeing Commercial Airplane Company constitute an Advisory Group on management development programmes, policies and activities.

16 December 1987

General Motors Corporation: Management Education Training and Development

1   The General Motors Corporation (GM) is the largest company in the world, with annual sales of $100 billion. The company has 876 000 employees world-wide. It follows that its approach to management education and training is of great interest.

2   GM has two main sources of managers – existing staff and the new graduate intake. All prospective managers (i.e., including first-line supervisors whom GM see as managers) who are non-graduates receive 8–26 weeks of full-time training. New first-line supervisors are all required to take a one-week full-time course; plus a second week when they become second-line; and a third week when they become departmental heads. The majority of tutors are from outside the company but this is in the process of change: GM see considerable advantages in using their own staff as tutors.

3   GM recruited 2000 graduates in 1984 but this number declined sharply in recent years. Another change in graduate recruitment is that the company became more selective in the universities from which it recruited. Experience had shown that the past practice of recruiting from some 600 universities had been of limited success: the policy now is to recruit from only 55 carefully selected universities. GM do not 'go overboard' for MBA graduates but see a useful role for the 200 or so they recruit each year. They also encourage appropriate members of staff to study part-time for the MBA degree and meet their tuition costs.

4   An interesting view expressed by some GM senior managers is that they are concerned lest the correct emphasis on good academic background will close down all the opportunities for the good man to progress to management from the shopfloor. It is obvious to many that this 'window' is closing rapidly.

5   Training goes all the way up the management tree. One new three-day course for senior executives on appointment was instituted in 1985, and a second one-week course was introduced in 1986. The tutors in these courses are mainly vice-presidents of the company and the chairman or the president also take part. Over 800 senior executives took

part in these courses in 1987. In both courses, top executives emphasize the corporate outline with quality the No. 1 objective and cost control very important. One comment made by the 'tutors' (i.e., top executives) is that those promoted to the senior ranks (5000 in these grades) were 'no longer the tenant – but now the landlord'.

6   It is obvious that GM give a high priority to education and training for all staff – including managers. There is seen to be an increasing need for managers to 'look outwards' and this is being met by training, e.g., role playing in how to deal with the press. The annual appraisal exercise also stimulated training; as part of this exercise managers are required to report on the training needs of subordinate managers and, subsequently, on how they have been met.

7   Precise details of the total expenditure and time spent on training across the corporation are not available as much of the responsibility for training is devolved to divisions and plants. However, for the USA, much central guidance and teaching materials (including interactive videos) have been developed and made available throughout the corporation. The extent of GM's expenditure on education and training generally is underlined by a September 1985 statement by the president of the corporation who said that 'given the scope of GM's educational activities, we could well become one of the largest non-public educational institutions anywhere within the next decade'.

4 January 1988

Management Education Training and Development in IBM

IBM's commitment to the education and training of its personnel is well known: perhaps less well known is the extent of the commitment. The company spends $800 million annually on education and training and, when the salaries of trainees are added to this, the total figure is in the region of $2 billion. Even the lower figure amounts to 1.6 per cent of turnover and $2000 (c. £1250) per employee. On any given day some 20 000 IBM people will be attending courses with some 4 ½ million student days a year.

   The company's dedication to education and training goes back a long way. In September 1933 the founder of the business – Thomas J. Watson Senior said, 'Progress in business today depends on education'. This view persists in the 1980s with the chairman of the IBM board – John R. Opel – confirming that 'Education is an IBM tradition. Every chairman of IBM has recognized the critical importance of helping people to develop themselves to their fullest potential'.

The general statistics on the company are significant. It employs some 400 000 people in 132 countries. Annual sales are over $50 billion and it has a similar amount in assets. The company (world-wide) has 52 500 managers (37 000 at first-line level, 14 000 at middle level and 1500 at executive level). It follows that the training and development of managers is seen by IBM as a vital part of their overall training programme. Much of the training for IBM's managers is carried out at the company's impressive Management Development Centre (MDC) at Armonk, Westchester County, New York. The MDC – opened in 1979 – is located in an attractive wooded site near the company's corporate headquarters some 30 miles north of New York City. The location is important in that it enables the senior officers of IBM – including the chief executive officer – to take an active role in the senior-level courses.

Each year some 5000 managers attend the 180-bedroom MDC residential courses: about half of them being new managers, one-third of them middle managers and the remainder attending senior-level courses, e.g. the International Executive Class.

The MDC follows the general IBM policy of, as far as practicable, using company staff as tutors. These are normally people serving on a 2–3 year stint as tutors on secondment from their regular duties. However, the company also has academics, consultants and government representatives as lecturers for some sessions – particularly for the senior and middle-level courses.

Course content varies according to the level of the participant. Much of the syllabus for new managers is devoted to 'people management' (communications, the appraisal system, managing performance problems, etc.). It is clear that the new managers are being provided with practical help, i.e., 'how to do it'. Indeed, one aim is that the course teaching can be put into effect on the Monday following the trainee's attendance at an MDC course. Each new manager in the USA is required to attend a 'new managers' school within 30 days of taking up his appointment and he will have a divisional-level 40-hour up-date each year thereafter. The content of the divisional courses is guided by a 'needs analysis'.

Middle managers' courses also include some practical teaching (performance planning and evaluation, the appeals process, etc.) but they are wider in course-content, with case studies and outside speakers.

Senior-level courses include the two-week 'Advanced Management School' for managers with the potential to fill executive positions. One important objective in these courses is thorough understanding of trends in the outside world which affect the company.

IBM's corporate goals are:

1   'To enhance our customer partnerships
2   To exhibit leadership in all products and services
3   To grow with the industry
4   To be efficient in everything we do
5   To sustain our profitability'.

The company believes that to meet these goals it will need an increasing supply of informed, skilful managers and executives. The IBM training programmes are clearly directed to these ends.

4 January 1988

Michigan State University

1   Michigan State University (MSU) is a massive establishment in central Michigan with a student population of over 41 000, an annual budget of $500 million, and excellent facilities including three swimming pools, two 18-hole golf courses and a 76 000-seat football stadium. The student total is over twice the student population of Oxford and Cambridge combined. It might be noted that MSU alumni hold top positions in many parts of public and business life in the USA.

2   The College of Business is by far the largest of the 16 MSU colleges with over 7500 students. It offers programs in business administration, economics and in the management of 'the feeding, housing and recreational sectors of the service industries'.

3   There are problems in recruiting professors for business schools. It is laid down that three-quarters of teaching staff must have a 'terminal' degree but because the other places are reserved for graduate assistants and similar (usually studying for a PhD) in practice all recruits for full teaching posts at MSU had to be PhDs.

4   The largest single group of students in the Business School are the 2200 majors in general business. This course is designed primarily for those going into a family business, or who wish someday to establish a business, or those going on to graduate work in business or law.

5   Next in size is accounting with 1400 majors. These students spend two years in 'general' studies and two years in accounting. Only a handful want to obtain a PhD (about three a year) and these usually go to jobs other than teaching. While they could now start (early/mid 20s) at $50 000 in teaching for the 9-month year with (say) another $11 000 to give $61 000 as an academic starting salary, the rewards in outside accounting could be much greater – if not on starting, certainly within a few years. A good PhD would certainly expect a partnership at (say) $135 000 a year at age 30/35 in the outside world.

6   At the time of visit there was a review of the curriculum under way for accounting degrees. The 'customer' wanted more management content. At present about ten per cent of the accounting degree is formally in 'management' but a great deal of accounting, e.g., auditing is, in practice, closely related to management.

7   The third largest group in the Business School are the 1100 students on the graduate course in hotels and catering – described as hotel, restaurant and institutional management (HRI). Sixty per cent of the enrolment is female. The success of the MSU courses is shown by the fact that there are nearly three job offers for every HRI graduate (360 a year) and over 90 per cent of them are placed. The 4000 alumni hold important positions in the hotels and catering industry.

8   An interesting point is that 30 per cent of those starting out on their HRI undergraduate work expressed the wish to become entrepreneurs in the catering industry but on graduation only 1–2 per cent took this view. This was probably related to the fact that – partly in response to the industry's needs – each graduate had to show proof of 800 hours' on-the-job experience in hotels/restaurant work. Once they had first-hand experience, the attractiveness of being a hotel/catering entrepreneur obviously became less attractive.

9   Graduate studies are provided in a wide range of studies from accounting to hotel and restaurant management. MSU has some 600

MBA students. Every one of them is usually required to complete satisfactorily a 'required core' of study in managerial accounting; decision-making models; organization and administration; marketing models, theories and strategies; financial decision making; macroeconomic models; and in administrative policy (in some cases exceptions can be made to this when students can show significant background in the subject or are taking one of these as a major course of study). The student will also do two elective courses and a 20-credit 'area of major concentration'.

10   The relevance of the core program is clear when the MSU MBA course at Troy, Michigan is considered. About 60 people a year enter this two-year part-time course and they include a wide range of managers and supervisors – even vice-presidents from small businesses. Normal entrants are expected to have at least ten years' business experience including a significant period with managerial responsibilities. The students continue in their normal full-time jobs but they are expected to attend classes for 8 hours a week and to study in their own time for 18–25 hours a week. The drop-out rate is low: this might be related to the fact that students are usually nominated by their companies who invariably pay the tuition costs and agree that work assignments will not interfere with the formal teaching. The pressures to succeed are obvious. Since the course started in 1964 it has been supported by over 350 employers who have sponsored over 1100 graduates. Over 130 Chrysler managers have been through this MBA program and so have a good cross-section of today's managers (supervisors, project engineers, plant managers and vice-presidents) from the other major vehicle manufacturers in nearby Detroit.

11   Apart from their normal course work the Troy MBA students have the opportunity to participate in an overseas visit at the midway point in their course. In 1986 the visit was a study-tour to China and Japan.

12   On 'new' teaching methods, MSU was the first USA university to use TV for teaching students. Some 20 years ago a 'master' TV lecture on an 'Introduction to Accounting' was shown to the sudents: the use was heavily criticized. Today 1200 students see the lecture, and MSU has the highest CPA pass rate. Students are free to choose a 'live' lecture or see it on TV: many choose the latter. Other aspects of new teaching

technology are used or being considered for the business school. For the future, satellite projection of lectures by 'important' people (those who command high fees) are likely to become increasingly common.

13   In addition to the undergraduate and graduate studies MSU provides a wide range of short courses for managers. These are of 1-day to 5-weeks duration and each year about 6000 people attend them.

4 FRANCE

BY COLIN GORDON

HISTORY AND CULTURE

Since the days of Louis XIV, the State in France has been omnipresent and omniscient. Indeed, Louis' all-powerful minister Jean-Baptiste Colbert, gave his name to the notion of *colbertisme*, a term synonymous with *dirigisme* (from the French verb *'diriger'* to run or manage), the idea that the State, in its wisdom, knows best and therefore leads, directs and controls. Its long arm can and does penetrate every aspect not only of political and economic activity, but also of industrial and social life. In this respect, France can be considered to be the most centrally regulated of all the Western democracies, a fact virtually unaltered, even enhanced by its Revolution.

Its institutions reflect this. Its most obvious manifestation occurred under the previous Socialist government (1981–1986) with the nationalization of vast sectors of industry and almost the whole of the banking sector. The tide has since turned as France, too, has succumbed to the vogue of privatization but nevertheless its old centralizing institutions remain intact. The finance ministry is a supreme example, directing much industrial policy as well as fiscal and monetary policy and a subordinate central bank. The French president has arguably more power in his own country than the Heads of State of most other Western countries have in theirs, and a Planning Commission, although its star is now on the wane, is still a powerful think tank.

To provide administrators and engineers to run it and build its infrastructure, the State created its own professional training establishments (called *grandes écoles*), quite separate from the universities, considered to be ill-suited for the purpose. Its supply of administrators and engineers was thus controlled, and entailed selection which resulted in the establishment of a fiercely competitive élite, well-compensated in terms of prestige, power and remuneration for their loyal service and who inevitably in turn were both by nature and education *dirigiste* or *colbertiste* in outlook.

With the growth of industry, the élite spread its wings and alighted as managers in the main bastions of the private sector. Having a foot in both camps, the system therefore provided the top echelons for both State service and private and public enterprises and bred a high degree of understanding and co-operation between them. It is not unusual to find a senior ex-civil servant at the head of a major bank or industrial company (but rarely is anyone from private industry co-opted into the Civil Service).

The preference of the best brains has always been for public service, though, and the élitist tradition long existed against a background of widely felt antipathy to industry and the notion of profit. There has been a perceptible sea-change, however, and a new enthusiasm has been generated for industry, largely as the result of the U-turn by the previous Socialist government in the early 1980s and its insistence that industry and not the State, should provide wealth and jobs. The very best of the élite still cling to the State, but a growing majority of the rest are turning to business for the excitement and adventure perceived as partially the result of Thatcherism and Reagonomics, which have had a considerable influence on the business scene and its main players in France. Although engineering schools still have the edge in the popularity stakes, business schools are enjoying more and more of the limelight.

Particular intellectual qualities mark this élite, pointing to another long tradition in France. Ever since Descartes and his advocacy in the seventeenth century of a more systematically analytical approach to science, a brand of intellectualism has prevailed which prizes rationality, synthesis and logical thinking. These and numeracy are the qualities most sought in the professional education and training dispensed in the engineering and business schools. Given this tendency, it is perhaps therefore not surprising to find that mathematics forms the main selection criterion for the *grandes écoles*. Coupled with the intense competition to be admitted to these schools the result is that the educational process tends to throw up brilliant problem-solving individuals expending their energy on jockeying for positions to gain authority and advantage in the bureaucratic hierachies of the administration and some of the larger, indigenous French companies. The call for more liberalism, less State intervention, the influence of the American multinational corporate model and a greater emphasis on entrepreneurship may be changing these qualities, too, however and it is against this background that professional education and training, not just that of managers, but also of all levels of employee, is the subject of intense debate in France.

THE EDUCATION SYSTEM

Introduction

Every year engineering schools produce some 13 500 students and business schools some 4500 students. These schools are not seriously threatened. They award a qualification which enjoys great value and esteem in the labour market, so much so that each graduate can expect to receive at least four to five job offers at annual salaries ranging from 115 000 francs to 220 000 francs (£11 500 to £22 000). To a lesser, but increasing, extent the universities too provide France's future managers. At the other end of the scale, one-third of an age group leaves the schooling system without any qualifications and 40 per cent of the unemployed are in the 16 to 25 age group. At all levels the education system is hyperselective (except, ironically and problematically for admission into the universities) and, although there is a general consensus of opinion that this system does and must provide quality at the top end, there is growing concern for those who are excluded, who 'fail' because they do not get through the selection process. This concern is intensified by a general awareness that in a world of increasingly fierce competition, competence is a key factor.

Compulsory secondary education

Secondary education is divided into two cycles. The first cycle is compulsory and is given in comprehensive schools called *collèges*. This lasts approximately from the age of 11 to the age of 15, provided there has been no repeat year. After a process called orientation pupils proceed to the next two-year stage. This point is critical for it will determine whether a pupil will be able to proceed to follow the 'general' education path or will be routed into an alternative system with a much greater vocational bias. Those taking the general route will receive at the end of the period spent in the *collège* a *Brevet d'Études du Premier Cycle* (BEPC), awarded on the basis of continuous assessment. The vocational system involves transfer (by some 12 per cent of 14-year-olds) to a *Lycée d'Enseignement Professionnel* (LEP) where pupils take a three-year course in a choice of three hundred subjects leading to the craft qualification *Certificat d'Aptitude Professionnelle* (CAP).

Orientation at the end of the preparation stage arouses much passion because it is perceived as a form of selection and leads to a considerable number of pupils (16.3 per cent in 1984–5, 14.4 per cent in 1983–4) repeating the second year of secondary school because the CAP alternative enjoys little prestige and is associated with what the French call 'selection by failure'. Parents and pupils alike view the LEP as some kind of social dustbin, as the source of ultimate humiliation in status terms. 'You'll go to the LEP' is viewed as a dire threat.

Although the CAP provides training in a multitude of skills, many of these are now no longer relevant to modern industry's needs and there is strong criticism of vocational, particularly technical, education in France at this level. One belief is that a quantitative increase is an answer. Unemployment amongst those with a CAP, however, increased between 1978 and 1984, underlining the argument that more vocational education does not, in itself, guarantee less unemployment, especially in a climate of uncertainty over which skills are required for the future and for which jobs. The general tendency is for French firms to recruit those with higher, less narrow qualifications which allow greater mobility and transfer.

Post compulsory secondary education

This is the secondary education second cycle and can take the form of either a short or a long course.

For the short course, some 23 per cent aged 15+ join the vocational *lycée* (LEP) for the two-year version of the CAP or the '*Brevet d'Études Professionnelles*' (BEP). This is more broadly based than the CAP.

The longer courses last three years and lead to the award of the *baccalauréat*. They are taken in *lycées* some of which are designated *lycée technique* in which the *baccalauréat de technicien* is taken. For those with this qualification, the alternatives are direct entry into industry or access to higher technician qualifications. The aim of both types of *lycée* is to provide an initial base of 'general culture' in the first year (including

French, History, Geography, Mathematics, Sciences and Foreign Languages) before students proceed to greater specialization in the second and third year. Theoretically, students have a choice of specialization in the general *lycée* at the end of the first year, but in practice, unless they have chosen the right optional subjects they are allowed, the system tends towards selective compartmentalization. As is so often the case in this one-start society, failure to make the right choice or to triumph over the selection process can be very costly. Early mistakes and failures are hard to rectify.

Thirty-eight per cent of an age group reach *baccalauréat* level with 29.4 per cent succeeding. Overall, some 54 per cent of the 16 to 18 age group stay on for some form of further general or vocational education. The previous government's aim was to increase the number of pupils gaining the *baccaulauréat* to 80 per cent of an age group by the year 2000, with the availability of a *baccalauréat général, baccalauréat technique* and a *baccalauréat professionnel*, the latter being increasingly accessible to those with the CAP. Yet some see the over-emphasis on the vocational side as misleading and cite the Japanese model, where even for car workers a more general *baccalauréat* is preferred. In the French context, however, with its insistence on qualifications, any diploma, even vocational (there are even shops providing false *baccalauréat* certificates), is worth more than none at all, although one official view expressed was that the idea of three *baccalauréats* rather than two was ridiculous and would inevitably lead to more people going nowhere, with job offers lagging well behind the annual educational throughput. Consequently, attention is now focusing on the *baccalauréat général* and *baccalauréat technique* and the debate on vocational courses continues.

Higher education

Higher education is provided in universities, *grandes écoles* and other institutions (some of which are private). A *baccalauréat* gives automatic entry to university, usually to a student's local university, where courses comprise three cycles. The first, lasting two years, leads to a general university studies diploma, the *Diplôme d'Études Universitaires Générales* (DEUG) which covers both compulsory and optional subjects. The second cycle also lasts two years, the first of which leads to the *licence* (approximate Bachelors) and the second to the *maîtrise* (Masters). The third cycle involves either three years leading to a doctorate or a one-year *Diplôme d'Études Supérieures Spécialisées* (DESS) in a highly specialized area.

The *grandes écoles* are specialized institutions to which entry is competitive by means of a *concours* (entrance examination) after two years of highly pressurized preparatory classes. In these the emphasis for the engineering and business schools is essentially on mathematics, eligibility for the classes for those schools being mainly determined by having the *baccalauréat C* (mathematics and physical sciences).

Most of the engineering schools have a scientific or technological speciality but some, including the Polytechnique (the foremost engineering school), are more generalist in emphasis and hence many engineers in industry have not only a scientific but a broader educational background.

The *Instituts Universitaires de Technologie* (IUT) are specialized scientific, business studies and technical institutions which were founded in 1969 to respond to the growing need for a shorter specialized technician course. They can be seen hierarchically as situated between the *baccalauréat* and the longer higher education courses available in the universities and *grandes écoles*. The IUT's offer a two-year course leading to the *Diplôme Universitaire de Technologie* (DUT). In 1982–3 there were some 54 000 full-time students. In the State and private *lycées techniques* there are also two-year courses available leading to a qualification similar to the DUT. This is the *Brevet de Technicien Supérieur* (BTS) in which there are some 124 specialisms. The objective is to provide these BTS courses in all the *lycées techniques* (approximate equivalents to the DUT and BTS would be the HND/BTEC in the UK). In the main, holders of the DUT and BTs are recruited at the supervisory (*Agent de Maîtrise*) and technician grades.

Thirty-five cent of an age group will go on to higher education, 66 per cent of which will enter university. Full figures for the Higher Education population are given in Table 4.1.

Diplomas

All qualifications referred to hitherto, both in secondary and higher education, would carry the generic label of *diplôme* in French. Higher levels of qualification are often designated by reference to the number of years the course lasts after the *baccalauréat*, e.g.: bac (*baccalauréat*) + 2 for DUT, BTS and DEUG; bac + 4 for a *maîtrise* or some business school diplomas (increasingly bac + 5); and bac + 5 for engineering schools and DESS.

Table 4.1: University population

	1982/3	1983/4
CPGE + STS	120527	137030
Universities:		
Law and economics	199789	200504
Arts	286637	291151
Sciences	142772	148428
Medicine	188074	187780
Multi-disciplinary	33239	37290
IUT	55314	57817
Total Universities:	905825	922970
Engineering schools	39000	40412
Business schools	23317	24578
Total	1088669	1124990

CPGE – Classes préparatoires aux grandes écoles
STS – Sections de techniciens supérieurs (leading to BTS)
Source: French Ministry of Education

THE FRENCH MANAGER

The term *cadre* will be generally used to denote the category of 'manager' in a French context although with some important modifications. This poses a number of complex problems since the two are by no means strictly equivalent and have sociological and legal connotations of an entirely different order in each country. In the sense, however, that the English word is generic, and can be qualified by 'trainee', 'senior', etc., and, similarly, in French, the word *cadre* can be expanded to *cadre débutant* (trainee manager), *cadre dirigeant/supérieur* (senior manager), there is an approximation which is close enough for the purposes of definition. The differences are of interest, however, and merit further exploration.

The word *cadre* as a concept in the business world first appeared in France in 1936 to designate engineers and others enjoying some level of authority, who, following the industrial unrest of the period, wished to assert their position and status in negotiations as a separate category distinct from that of heads of companies on the one hand and workers on the other.

Legal recognition followed after the Second World War in the form of the Parodi–Croizat decrees of 1946 which provided for two categories of cadre:

1   Those who without having any command function have acquired technical training (*formation*) generally leading to a diploma and who applied their set of knowledge in their job.

2   Any person having acquired either technical, administrative, legal, commercial or financial training and who exercises some form of command, delegated to them by their employer, over other employees.

The first category includes engineers who generally, but not necessarily, would have a diploma; the second includes those with a different type of training (no mention being made of diplomas) who have some form of command function.

These distinctions can now still be seen in collective bargaining agreements and form the main difference between the concept of management grades in Britain and France. In the latter, management status and salary are graduated as precisely as in a military setting (hence the word *cadre*, borrowed from the army). They are part of a strict hierarchy covering all levels of employment and are sanctioned by labour legislation. Additionally, these definitions are important in the sphere of social legislation since they are those used (together with an important modification made in 1982 to include supervisory grades and technicians and called *encadrement*) firstly for the purpose of the institution of industrial tribunals and, secondly, for pension rights. The British system is informal and much looser and the term of manager has no legal status.

Interestingly, the French occasionally also use the English word 'manager' but this is restricted to someone in senior management who would be expected to take major decisions which might commit the company.

There are a number of ways of becoming a *cadre*. Firstly, a graduate with no professional experience can be appointed directly to a position of *cadre*, but only at the bac + 4/5 level. Secondly, employees may come up through the ranks and become *cadre*. In such cases, the promotion will be based on a combination of experience, qualifications and seniority. Those with a technician grade could expect, for example, to become a *cadre* after a period of four to five years, whereas a skilled worker with no formal *ingénieur* qualifications could become *ingénieur-maison* (company engineer) only after a considerable number of years of experience. The latter are generally referred to as *autodidacte* (self-taught) and may or may not have any other qualifications than a CAP or at best a *baccalauréat*. Chances of reaching top management for the latter are very limited in large companies where diplomas are increasingly important and correspond fairly strictly to set levels within the corporate hierarchy.

Qualifications and cadres

Overall, just less than 30 per cent of each generation succeed in obtaining a *baccalauréat*. Some 21 per cent of the total working population possess at least the *baccalauréat*. Forty-five per cent have no diploma at all but there are wide variations in industry according to sector.

The sectoral concentration of those with a higher education diploma can be seen in Table 4.2. The service sector takes some three-quarters of those with a higher qualification with only some 16.2 per cent in industry. This is not a new situation and is partly due to the fact that the civil service has traditionally recruited higher diploma graduates in large numbers. Approximately one-third are teachers (classified as civil servants in France) but nevertheless an acute imbalance is clearly perceptible.

Table 4.2: Sectoral percentage of Higher Education Diplomas

Sector	Numbers employed (%)	Higher Education Diplomas (%)
Services	37.8	73.6
Industry	35.3	16.2

Table 4.3 shows the percentage of *cadres* possessing qualifications of *baccalauréat* or higher, both by sex and as a whole. The terminology here is the more precise definition used by the INSEE (National Statistics Office), *cadres d'entreprise*, which is a subheading of the group *cadres et*

professions intellectuelles supérieures and would not include the supervisory grades, technicians, etc. There are some 996 000 *cadres d'enterprise*, i.e.: 4.5 per cent of the working population.

Table 4.3: Percentage of cadres qualified to baccalauréat or higher

	Male			Female		All	
Qualification	Number qualified	% of total males cadre	Number qualified	% of total females cadre	Number qualified	% of all cadre
Bac	168 692	19.9	28 707	18.0	197 399	19.8
Bac + 2	101 935	12.0	20 987	13.8	122 922	12.3
Bac + 4/5	316 774	37.5	49 353	32.5	366 127	36.6
Total Bac (+)	587 401	69.4	99 047	64.3	686 448	68.7

Source: INSEE, *Enquête sur l'emploi,* March 1985

Some of the conclusions are quite clear and worth underlining. Overall some 69 per cent of *cadres,* using the narrower INSEE definition, have at least the *baccalauréat* and some 37 per cent have a bac + 4/5 qualification (*grandes écoles* or four plus years in a university). These figures are for industry as a whole and there will be considerable variations according to company size and industrial sector. In companies with a turnover in excess of one billion francs, 90 per cent of general managers will have a higher education qualification (at least bac + 4), according to a recent report by Neumann International. None will be *autodidacte,* the remaining having acquired some form of qualification during their working lives. At the very top, two thirds will be graduates of engineering schools, but the top business schools are making serious inroads into the privileged fiefs of the engineers.

One noticeable trend over the last 15 years has been the increase in the number of those with a diploma from the shorter higher education cycle (DUT/BTS) and the increasing competition they represent for lower levels of management with those employees rising from the ranks with either no diploma or *baccalauréat* level only.

MANAGEMENT EDUCATION AND DEVELOPMENT

Pre-entry education

ENGINEERING SCHOOLS

In France, engineers occupy the highest number of top management posts, a position virtually unchanged and unchallenged until the arrival on the scene of competing business schools. Engineers not only fill senior technical positions (and would-be heads of manufacturing companies) but they are very much in competition with other specialists (economists and lawyers from the universities, and graduates from business schools) and frequently their jobs no longer retain a technical or scientific nature, but are oriented towards administration and general management. They are to be found not only in the manufacturing sector, but also, and increasingly, in banking and finance. They form a mafia and many a large company (e.g.: SNCF, Elf-Aquitaine, Renault, Peugeot) has positions reserved specifically for students of certain engineering schools (particularly Polytechnique).

It is important, therefore, that the origins of the engineering schools in France are understood. Although some 30 per cent of *diplômes d'ingénieur* are awarded by establishments having a status close to that of universities, there has always been an historic and unique separation between a professionally-oriented form of education and the more classical university system. Back in the eighteenth century, the universities were considered too mediaeval and ivory-towered and they were little interested in any practical application of their teachings or research. Set up as long ago as the eleventh century, they slid into serious decline in the sixteenth century and, unlike the universities in Great Britain and Germany, were bypassed by the great movement of ideas which transformed Western Europe. One of their greatest sins was to be independent, and so the Revolution, in typical centralizing fashion, put paid to this by abolishing them. Napoleon mistrusted their freedom, too, upheld their abolition and indeed it was not until 1896 that the title 'university' was restored.

Meanwhile, however, the State required engineers and civil servants to look after its own particular technical and administrative interests. It created the first engineering schools, the first being the *École des Ponts et*

Chaussées (for civil engineering) in 1775 and the *École des Mines* (originally for mining but now for all sectors of industry). Together with the schools there appeared in French administration the *Grands Corps*, which resemble collegiate bodies acting as old-boys' clubs and dominating selection of the upper echelons of the civil service. Their most significant function is to provide State and industry with a constant stream of the best talent, both technical and administrative. They are the last word in closed shops and have long typified the vested interests and corporatism of the French administration, although many would defend their record in helping build the French economy in the 1960s and 1970s through their achievements in the aerospace, nuclear, armaments and telecommunications industries.

BUSINESS SCHOOLS

A number of commercial schools had existed since the nineteenth century. In the provinces they were established by local Chambers of Commerce which play such a prominent part both in initial business education (*formation initiale*) and in continuing education (*formation continue*). These schools concentrated on basic 'technical' skills such as law and accounting. In Paris at that time, there also existed the three major present-day business schools, which are part of the *grandes écoles* system: the *École des Hautes Études Commerciales* (HEC), the *École Supérieure des Sciences Économiques et Commerciales* (ESSEC) and the *École Supérieure de Commerce de Paris* (ESCP); although still only 'commercial' schools they were founded as a complement to the engineering schools and in their structure, particularly their methods of rigorous entry selection by *concours*, they closely paralleled the aims and objectives of the engineering schools. Indeed, the selection procedure is still very similar, with the *baccalauréat C* group of subjects (mathematics and science) being by far the principal means of entry.

It was not until after 1945, in fact at the beginning of the 1960s, with the concentration of industry and the influx of both American capital and business ideas that there started a movement towards the foundation of 'business' schools, and in greater numbers, particularly in the regions (as with most other things, the *grandes écoles* being particularly concentrated in Paris). Chambers of Commerce were prominent in this movement and sent hundreds of their members to America to study American business methods. At the same time, influential business men were suggesting the creation of French equivalents to Harvard, Wharton and Massachusetts Institute of Technology (MIT). Although American industry itself was seen as a great threat to French industry, a fact which led to France treading its fiercely independent line in the aerospace, nuclear and other

Table 4.4: Salaries paid in relation to qualifications held

Qualifications	Annual salaries (000s francs)		
	Minimum	Mean	Maximum
Engineering/scientific graduates			
Grande école scientifique + Harvard/MIT/INSEAD	130	167	220
Polytechnique	130	160	200
Grandes écoles d'ingénieurs	130	156	190
Arts et métiers	117	150	186
ENSI (IDN, CESTI, ESIEE, ENSEM, ENSEEHT)	117	143	186
INSA Lyon	117	141	186
Doctorat maths/sciences	120	144	186
DEA maths/sciences	110	141	186
Maîtrise maths/sciences	100	138	186
Pharmacy/medicine	130	147	186
Pharmacy/medicine + business studies	130	147	186
Business graduates			
Grande école commerciale + Harvard/MIT/INSEAD	127	157	195
HEC	117	150	190
ESSEC	117	148	186
Political science (IEP Paris)	117	142	186
Ecole supérieure de commerce de Paris	117	144	186
ESCAE – Provinces	100	135	186
EAP	100	138	186
Other			
DECS (accounting)	106	136	186
Doctorat (troisième cycle) business studies/law	110	135	186
DEA business studies/law	106	132	186
Maîtrise business studies/economics/law	106	129	186

Source: Figaro, October 1986
Note: Exchange rate for sterling equivalents at March 1986 is 9.7 francs to the pound.

fields, there was a vast wave of enthusiasm for American management methods. This is echoed even today by the value companies place on graduate recruits with an American qualification, particularly an MBA. From the salaries in Table 4.4 it will be seen that there is a clear premium placed on qualifications acquired from *both* engineering/business schools *and* Harvard, MIT and INSEAD (not part of the French business school system and awarding an MBA, which is not officially recognized in France by the Ministry of Education). Furthermore, the majority of the faculty in the major business schools (ESSEC, HEC, ESCP and Lyon) have an MBA, MSc or PhD from an American university or business school. In many cases, an Anglo-Saxon PhD is seen as clearly more desirable than a French state doctorate and promotion may depend on its acquisition.

Table 4.5: Distribution of 'A' Level students by subject groups

General **baccalauréat**	**67.8%**
Bac A Arts	18.1%
Bac B Economics	14.2%
Bac C Maths/sciences	13.7%
Bac D Maths/natural sciences	18.9%
Bac E Science and technical	2.6%
Technical **baccalauréat**	*32.2%*
Bac F Industrial techniques/medico-social/music/dance	14.2%
Bac G Administration, business studies, commerce	17.2%
Bac H Computers	0.5%

Today there are just over 20 business schools in France which can claim the title of *grande école* since they recruit by *concours* (open entrance examination) after two years of *classes préparatoires* (preparatory classes given in specialist *lycées*). Selection remains severe since there are, for example, some 3000 candidates each year for only 250–300 places at ESSEC and HEC.

At the heart of the *grandes écoles* system lies the idea of rigorous selection based on mastery of quantitative techniques, on rapid problem-solving and on abstract mathematical reasoning. This has long been accepted as the only 'fair' way of testing for ability. It is defended because any other means is likely to be more vague and less impartial. Its critics are numerous, however, and whilst accepting the need for engineers to be strong in mathematics (and the strongest almost exclusively choose engineering schools), they believe that, in the case of business schools, such an excessively narrow, maths-based system (97 per cent of successful candidates have the Maths Bac C whereas overall only 13.7 per cent taking the *baccalauréat* have the Bac C, Table 4.5) perpetuates the élitist tradition, and provides no safety net for those who may have qualities such as imagination and creativity which are every bit as vital to the successful manager. Some of the business schools do indeed accept people with other backgrounds (law, medicine, etc., studied at the universities in the French system) directly into the second of a three-year programme, but these too will have to show great strength in mathematics (unkind tongues would say they chickened out of the 'royal way' to the top, i.e.: in the engineering and business schools).

Opponents of the dominance of mathematics go further and point to its exorbitant influence throughout the education system. At *baccalauréat* level, it can have the perverse effect of pushing pupils to follow a highly mathematical *baccalauréat* group of subjects even if they are aiming at studies in which maths are far from being fundamental. The Bac B concentrates on economics but to do a course of economic science, even accounting, at a university, the mathematics-based Bac C is almost *de rigueur*. Hence the mirage of the infamous Bac C.

Some lesser schools consider that the bar is placed too high and prefer to rely more on interviews, tests and school records in their search for more rounded candidates. Further, personality is of equal importance to numeracy and there are signs that there is a growing, albeit as yet ineffective, conviction that selection procedures must change and place more emphasis on individual qualities.

The *grandes écoles* selection procedure is not the only target of criticism, however. Quite recently a number of books (particularly *Tu seras président, mon fils* by Jean-Michel Gaillard) have added to the swelling chorus of those who would like to see drastic changes. One of the most common complaints, particularly amongst ex-students, is that the schools are too generalist and prepare jacks of all trades but masters of none. What is taught is out of step in its academic and theoretical rigidity with what is required in the modern world, is another cry. There is then the charge that the best talent is never attracted to take up research as a career, since this is almost exclusively the domain of the universities and therefore quasi-taboo (some would point to the paucity of Nobel Prize winners in France as evidence of this), and that in the words of one senior French manager, 'students go to the *grandes écoles* to acquire not knowledge and understanding, but a social status'. Even now, less than 5 per cent of *grandes écoles* students come from working class backgrounds, although selection methods in principle give an equal chance to all. In practice, the social make-up of the schools is self-perpetuating with students often being the latest in a long line of parents and grandparents who had the same advantage or generally coming from families well-versed in what is required to make it to the élite. Meritocratic in appearance, but the odds are heavily stacked against you, if you are a train driver's son.

All this adds up to a pretty fundamental denunciation of the system. Some would scrap the whole present structure and bring it more into line with what happens in the university sector in the USA, Great Britain and West Germany. But, however harsh the criticisms might be, no one is prepared to grasp the nettle. Those in a position to do so, politicians, civil servants, industrialists, are often themselves products of the system and, even if critical of many of its aspects, are viscerally attached to the quality it produces and the prestige it bestows, and form its most ardent defenders. For them, although they have shortcomings, the *grandes écoles* are irreplaceable and make up for the even greater deficiences of the universities. Élitist they may be, but the French scornfully point to the élites of Japan, the US and even the UK and see very little difference.

According to Dominique Xardel, the former Director of ESSEC, the business schools in particular have come a long way since the 1960s and have much to be proud of. In the 1960s, the emphasis in all of the business or commercial schools in France shifted away from the narrow concept of basic technical skills (*commerce*) towards adopting American business methods (*gestion*). Today, a further shift may be perceptible, a shift perhaps not totally unrelated to the first. In M. Xardel's words: 'Twenty years ago they were called *écoles de commerce*, ten years ago *écoles de gestion* and now *écoles de management*'. This latter term implies all the qualities inherent in the concept of leadership and decision-making. Indeed in ESSEC's brochure, *Les managers de demain*, the accent is on personal qualities, professionalism, rigour, a more international perspective and the ability to take decisions in a world of increasing uncertainty and constant adaptation to change.

Taxe d'apprentissage

The primary source of income for some private schools (two-thirds of the total in the case of ESSEC) is the *taxe d'apprentissage* (apprenticeship tax) which is levied on all companies employing more than 10 people, at the rate of 0.5 per cent of the gross wage bill. Twenty per cent of this must either be spent on internal apprenticeship schemes or go to external apprenticeship training centres. Seven per cent is paid to the Chambers of Commerce for expenditure on other forms of vocational technical training (of which they are major providers, the Paris Chamber, with a billion francs turnover, running alone seven establishments of business school level, seven at bac + 2 and 70 up to *baccalauréat* level). Companies have a choice of how to spend the remaining 73 per cent: directly to approved educational establishments (business or other vocationally oriented schools), to Chambers of Commerce which act as collecting and distributing agencies, or as a final resort to the Treasury (only some 6 per cent). In fierce competition with suppliers of education, organizations such as ESSEC employ their own tax 'hunters' to persuade both new companies to part with their contributions and existing patrons (such as Kodak, in the case of ESSEC) to remain faithful. What's in it for companies? Primarily, the useful and the practical, hence most entrepreneurs would pay to their old school, that of their son or of their future employees. Without openly saying so, companies might expect priority treatment when it comes to staff recruitment. They might provide work experience or consultancy projects for students – but in return, exert pressure to ensure the work is properly done. Some seek good publicity, requiring their logos to be positioned above the entrance to lecture theatres, demanding pole position for their stand during milkround exhibitions or expecting to be asked to provide staff to give lectures. Equipment is often supplied instead of handing over a cheque. This is quite legitimate, provided the equipment has a direct link with the education dispensed. Grass cutters for the school lawns are out, therefore, and goods must be given at cost.

UNIVERSITIES

It would be a mistake to believe that universities play no part in providing industry with its future managers and, indeed, in volume terms there are as many managers in industry as a whole with a university qualification as there are with a diploma from a *grande école*. This is hardly surprising since a glance at the comparative figures for the two systems in Table 4.1 will suffice to show that, given industry's present requirement for triple the number of *grandes écoles* students than are being produced, it has to turn to the universities. Table 4.6 gives a breakdown of managers' qualifications according to age-band and again demonstrates quite clearly that, apart from engineers who gain their qualification predominantly from the engineering schools, university qualifications are as much in evidence for non-technical posts as business school diplomas, a trend which increases the younger the age-band and points to the growing academization of management. This observation is particularly true of

Table 4.6: Diplomas in management posts

	Age Band		
	25–34 yrs	*35–44 yrs*	*45–54 yrs*
Grandes Ecoles et Diplôme d'Ingénieur			
Cadres administratifs et commerciaux des entreprises	21.1%	14.9%	12.3%
Ingénieurs	49.4%	36.2%	31.6%
2e et 3e Cycles Universitaires			
Cadres administratifs et commerciaux des entreprises	20.5%	11.4%	6.1%
Ingénieurs	11.2%	7.7%	3.0%
BTS – BUT			
Cadres administratifs et commerciaux des entreprises	12.3%	6.8%	2.9%
Ingénieurs	13.7%	11.9%	6.0%

E.g.: For every 100 engineers between 25 and 34 years old, 49.4% have a *grande école* diploma.
Source: Recensement de 1982. Volume Formation.

levels in the hierarchy requiring the BTS/IUT qualification (supervisory and technician grades).

Traditionally, universities have been non-selective and provided the bulk of the teaching profession, researchers, lawyers and doctors but, beginning in the early 1970s, various courses have been provided to allow students to follow professionally oriented courses geared to the needs of management. The University of Paris Dauphine was an important pioneer in this respect. In every case, however, the courses have a specific reference to the needs of industry. It is indeed a feature of the higher education field that the 'pure' arts graduate would have little or no chance of being employed in industry without a diploma from such a course.

Companies are bewildered, however, by the arcane complexity of this increasing multiplicity of new university qualifications and prefer to stick to the familiarity of the well-tried and tested homogeneity of the *grandes écoles* diplomas. If anything, the trend tends to some extent to reinforce companies' already deep-seated suspicion of the universities. They have traditionally been identified as breeding-grounds for left-wing revolt and sedition, and hence the very antithesis of the security of the *grandes écoles* which can be relied upon to produce loyal, order-loving and conservative managers.

The issue of selection in universities poses its problems, too. For companies, lack of selection spells greater uncertainty when recruiting: it is far easier and safer to interview four to five *grandes écoles* students to gain one recruit than see twenty university students and perhaps employ none. For the students themselves, no selection gives them another chance if they have already failed the *grandes écoles* selection hurdle. The system creaks with inefficiency, however, and cries out for some kind of selection process together with a clear identification of each university's strengths and weaknesses to help students in their choice and allocate resources where needed and justified. As it is, any holder of the *baccalauréat* has the right, on a first-come first-served basis, to a place at his or her local university. Prospective students, however bright, oversleep on registration day at their peril. But any official attempts to introduce selection are liable to suffer the fate witnessed in December 1986, when students took to the streets to demonstrate in time-honoured, revolutionary manner.

In reality, the university systems' contribution to management education is considerably greater than is generally believed. Mention has already been made of the actual number of university students in management. A great many members of faculties in the business schools are from the universities (there often being few permanent faculty members in the schools) and enjoy international acclaim. Most research comes from the universities and, finally, since the 1960s great efforts have been made to respond to industry's needs and vocationalize courses.

Whatever the strengths and weaknesses of the two systems, the large companies are still very much attached to the *grandes écoles* system as being the supplier of the best talent, certainly for its future senior managers. As a Thomson executive put it, 'We are at war with other international companies and therefore we are obliged to go for the best in qualifications. We must get the top-level *matière grise* (grey matter) and for this we turn to the Polytechnique, École Centrale, HEC, ESSEC, ESCP, etc.'. These are the words of a senior manager, an Englishman, at Procter and Gamble where it is the same story:

'We have to look for people who are going to go fast and develop into managers quickly. So we look for our *cadres* in the business schools, we orientate all our recruitment to these schools and stay in constant touch with them. We have a clear objective to go for the top ten schools, because that's where the best people are. In intellectual terms, they do turn out a high calibre of individual who can study a problem and come up quickly with an answer. From a business point of view they are streets ahead of UK students who haven't done a business degree.'

A view echoed by a Scotsman working at Price Waterhouse in Paris who considered the French manager better trained, although traditionally preferring to work in a different place, i.e.: in State administration.

Most frequently, then, companies assume that applicants for management posts have the necessary intellectual ability. However, a number of companies stress that the education received should be more action-oriented and practical. Whatever an applicant's qualifications, personal qualities are nevertheless seen to be of prime importance and these include the ability to learn from others and leadership. In particular M. Le Gorrec, the President of the French Association of Training Managers and Assistant Personnel Director of EDF-GDF (combined electricity and gas boards), made the point, 'French *cadres* are trained to be very rational and find it difficult when confronted with people older than themselves and with considerable work experience to accept that things are never perfect or completely solvable. It is difficult for them to manage people and it is therefore vital that they have a series of successive experiences other than formal training'. The fierce competition entailed in their education makes them highly individualistic and self-seeking. Many feel that life owes them a living: ironically, at Procter and Gamble, it was reckoned that they made more mistakes with students from some of the top business schools because of this. Consequently, recruitment procedures are getting tighter for the *grandes écoles* students who think their diploma is a passport to the top. Companies are expecting greater mobility too, with many demanding that their young managers accept to be moved around, not just from function to function, but also geographically. Young managers are slowly being compelled to undergo a change in mentality, to accept a framework of constraints within which the onus will be on them to manage their own career and not expect to sit back and have a safe, easy ride. This is becoming all the more acute as the employment market is beginning to show a downturn and competition is becoming keener.

Companies would like to see more done to change some of the focus in the business schools and in a joint report by Hay-France and FNEGE* in 1980 entitled *Horizon 85*, giving recommendations for the future teaching of management, senior managers gave their opinion on priorities management schools should be adopting:

- less emphasis on quantitative techniques;
- complete mastery of the use of computers;
- more emphasis on sales and selling;
- the training of multilingual managers.

Of students it said that:

- their general culture should concentrate on the main factors of change in the environment about them, both nationally and internationally. This would enable a better appreciation of global corporate strategy.
- As important as general culture is the learning of methods and in

*FNEGE (*Fondation Nationale pour l'Enseignement de la Gestion des Entreprises*) set up in 1968 to improve the teaching of management, funded by the government and the chambers of commerce and including in its membership the *grandes écoles* and the university institutes.

particular the development of intellectual discipline and the use of rigour.

Post-entry education and development

Since most students with a *baccalauréat* leave school at 18/19, the average age of new *cadres* to industry (bac + 4/5) is 24/25 for male students, after 12 months' compulsory military service, and 23/24 for female students. All will have completed 'stages' (industrial training periods) as an integral part of their course. The 'stage' system is almost institutionalized in French companies and is perhaps more widespread than in most other industrialized countries. In the case of ESSEC, for example, these 'stages' will number three, some four to five months in all, over a period of three years. In this connection, there is often a close relationship with the *petites et moyennes entreprises* (PME – small and medium-sized companies), for both 'stages' and teaching, although few ESSEC students would join a PME, feeling they deserve larger companies and salaries.

In addition, within the *grandes écoles* there are organizations called *junior-entreprises* which are school-based consultancies at the disposal of outside companies requiring expert help and advice in particular areas. These are popular with companies and in some cases turn over nearly a million francs a year. Sometimes they take the form of joint ventures between the engineering and business schools and would hence allow combined teams to look at projects from both a technical and a business angle. One such example is INGECOM which brings students of ESSEC together with those of the *École Supérieure d'Électricité*. This is of particular importance to the engineers, who receive relatively little management training and yet are expected to manage. The activities of the *junior-entreprises* are not the responsibility of the teaching staff, however, nor integrated in any way into academic studies. The organizations are completely autonomous and students are legally liable themselves for any possible problems.

RECRUITMENT

Procedures show a wide variation and, in the largest companies, would involve group interviews and exercises, plus psychological and other tests, including interestingly graphology on which increasing emphasis is being placed. There has been much talk recently of a return to schools producing an order of merit for their students, a system abolished in the 1970s. Such a classification has recently been reintroduced at ESSEC in the belief that it keeps pressure up on students who occasionally relax their efforts and try to coast through their studies once they have passed the all important entrance *concours*. Some companies believe it would enable quicker identification of the best potential, but in the main, most are not in favour and believe that since students give proof of their intellectual mettle by their very presence in a school, more reliance should be placed on their human qualities.

INDUCTION

Generally speaking, training for new graduates may vary from no formal training at all to highly systematic training. An example of such training is encountered in one of the major construction companies, SCREG, a subsidiary of BOUYGUES (one of the main contractors for the construction of the Channel Tunnel) where new engineers spend 12 to 15 months in four different regional divisions (a period interrupted in winter by four to five weeks of technical training in the company's new engineering school). For business students from HEC, ESSEC, etc., there is also a tour of various divisions during which time three-monthly periods are spent in key functional areas.

In Paribas, one week's initial training covers the bank's strategy, organization and background and top management is expected to be involved. Thereafter the young manager has a menu of optional courses from which to choose in the first year. In Procter and Gamble, however, recruits in the sales division are given their own personalized training programmes on the first day which is totally integrated into a target of set objectives.

In EDF–GDF, the first year is seen as a probationary year. New recruits get together for the first week to discuss the company's policy and strategy with top management. Thereafter, for technical *cadres*, there are six weeks during which to learn basic skills, e.g.: plumbing, fitting, etc., in the company's own school. Time must be spent in each functional area of the company and, after one year, they are taken in groups of fifteen to give them time to reflect, with top management, on the company's problems, e.g.: nuclear energy. This process is conducted and supervised by group leaders.

In Total, the trend has been to cut back on 'heavy' introductory courses and concentrate more on less abstract and less passive action-training. Managers are encouraged to train young trainees and put them into working groups to learn how to tackle problems.

Induction training is probably more common in American multinationals than in French companies which claim they cannot afford it and anyway tend to require students to be operational straightaway. 'In France, there is the feeling that once you've had your formal education, that's enough.' In many cases, however, this feeling exists because the education received in the *grandes écoles* is seen as too general and theoretical – 'You learn how to operate your brain, but not a company' – and hence a good dose of practical on-the-job experience is preferred to more formal training.

Continuing education (formation continue)

The main characteristics of the system are:

- Under various acts since 1971, it is financed by a training tax equal of 1.2 per cent of the gross wage bill and payable by all companies of more than 10 employees.
- Such companies must complete form 2483 showing details of training by cost, type, length, category and sex of employee, etc.
- 0.2 per cent of this tax (i.e.: 0.2 per cent of wage bill) goes directly to the Treasury to fund training schemes for the young unemployed.
- Companies of more than 50 employees must draw up a *plan de formation* (training plan) which is submitted and discussed with the *comité d'entreprise* (works committee). These discussions cover both the previous year and the year to come. All companies are also obliged to include the minutes of these discussions when sending form 2483 to the local tax authorities.
- In addition, every individual has the right to a *congé individuel de formation* (individual training leave). The company may defer permission, giving reasons, but for no longer than 12 months. The leave may not exceed one year if full-time. For this, the employee may receive up to 100 per cent of his/her salary.
- The *congé* is financed by a 0.1 per cent levy on the wage bill (deducted from the 1.2 per cent training tax) which is paid to special organiza-

tions charged with managing the financing of such *congés* (*Fonds d'Assurance Formation* (FAF) and *Fonds Paritaires de Gestion du Congé Individuel de Formation* (FONGECIF)).

Actual expenditure by companies on training in 1983 was 18 billion francs, with a provisional figure of 18.7 billion francs for 1984. This slender increase, when compared with the 15.6 billion recorded in 1982 and 13.2 billion in 1981, shows signs of serious stagnation and is almost certainly due to the effects of the policy of economic austerity implemented by the Socialist government in 1983. Unlike the Germans, it would seem that the French do not spend *more* on training during periods of hardship.

The total does not include all expenditure on management training which is estimated to be some 30 per cent of these totals although, in spite of the mass of statistics available on training in France, there are no reliable figures to support this particular point. This estimate is based on that of individual companies which quite regularly, however, fail to include some expenditure on management training in their tax declaration.

A breakdown of expenditure as a percentage of wage bill, by selected sectors and size of company for 1983 is given in Table 4.7. It quite clearly shows the lead being given by the State in the provision of training in the nationalized electricity, gas and transport sectors. This may well be due to the fact that these sectors are amongst the most heavily unionized and hence more pressure to train is brought to bear through the works committees when discussing the training plans.

Average expenditure on training per employee (in francs) is given in Table 4.8. The increases are particularly noticeable in the smaller companies and point to an increasing use and awareness of training in these companies, although as will be seen later, they face a number of problems.

Table 4.9 gives the percentage of employees benefiting from training by category, sex and size of company. Two points are worth making in this respect:

(a) Overall, approximately one third of the male technician/management grade benefit from training as opposed to 11 per cent for unskilled male workers.

Table 4.7: Breakdown of training expenditure as percentage of wages bill by selected sectors and size of company in 1983

Sector	Number of Employees					
	10-19	20-49	50-499	500-1999	2000+	Total
Electric and electronic industries	1.16	1.17	1.34	2.20	3.49	2.78
Mechanical engineering	1.01	1.09	1.27	1.74	1.66	1.40
Production and distribution of electricity, gas, etc.	1.99	1.43	2.18	1.80	6.84	6.39
Aeronautics, shipbuilding	0.92	1.11	1.42	1.56	1.84	1.75
Construction industry	1.11	1.13	1.16	1.37	1.17	1.18
Retail food industry	0.94	1.19	1.12	1.35	1.67	1.45
Transport	1.10	1.10	1.65	1.57	5.80	4.09
Insurance	1.08	1.55	1.91	2.62	3.34	2.86
Financial organizations, banks, etc.	1.88	1.93	2.54	3.35	3.81	3.44
Total (all industry and services)	1.10	1.17	1.47	1.94	3.36	2.14

Source: CEREQ, 1985

(b) The number of men trained is somewhat higher than women, although the situation is changing significantly.

An interesting point to note is that the smaller the company, the greater the chances women have of being trained. Indeed, in the 10–19 employee range of companies, a *higher* percentage of women is being trained across nearly all the grades, but particularly in management. This is also true of the next group (20–49) and even in the larger companies the figures are not significantly different. Reasons for this are unclear but could well have something to do with the provisions of the Roudy Act of July 1983 which will be examined later.

Statistics are also available on the numbers taking advantage of the *congé individuel de formation* (some 40,000 in 1983, 44 000 in 1984) and the regional distribution of training in terms of category, sex, age and size of company.

Table 4.8: Average expenditure on training per employee

No of employees in company	10-19		20-49		50-499		500-1999		2000+	
Year	1983	1984	1983	1984	1983	1984	1983	1984	1983	1984
Expenditure per employee (francs)	849	1026	920	1084	1207	1332	1780	2048	3331	3704
Increase of 1984 on 1983	20%		17.8%		10.3%		15%		11.2%	

Source: CEREQ, 1985

Table 4.9: Percentage of employees having followed training courses in 1984

No of employees in company	10-19		20-49		50-499		500-1999		2000+	
Sex	M	F	M	F	M	F	M	F	M	F
Unskilled, semi-skilled workers	3	2	3	2	7	5	11	9	22	10
Skilled workers	3	3	5	3	11	6	16	14	38	17
Office staff	6	7	8	9	15	15	27	24	40	31
Supervisory/ technician	10	12	14	16	24	24	37	32	52	46
Engineers/ managers	13	16	17	19	28	28	42	39	49	47

Source: CEREQ, 1985

These statistics are gathered and collated, on the basis of the 2483 declaration by CEREQ (*Centre d'Études et de Recherches sur l'Emploi et les Qualifications* – a government agency which publishes them yearly, together with numerous other reports and statistics on employment and qualifications). Analyses made are purely quantitative, however, and make no attempt to judge content or pass any qualitative opinion. The statistics are added as an appendix to the annual Finance Act, showing the level of training expenditure. In addition, they are used by the National Planning Commission (France having a series of five-year economic, social and cultural plans, the current one being the IXth, 1984–8) which is at present very much concerned with the whole area of continuing education.

ORGANIZATION OF TRAINING IN COMPANIES

Companies have a choice as to how the 0.8 per cent (after deduction from the 1.2 per cent of the 0.2 per cent for youth training and the 0.1 per cent for the individual training leave scheme) is to be spent:

(a) They can decide to provide their own training, internally or externally.
(b) They can enter into a contract with an external body such as:
    – a Chamber of Commerce
    – a consultancy
    – a sectorial or intersectorial trade association (the *Fonds d'Assurance Formation* (FAF) administered jointly by employers and the trade unions)
    – a private school or company (e.g.: a business school like ESSEC)
    – an individual or other association.

Figure 4.1 shows the use of funds by companies and Fig. 4.2 the various market shares held by the various training organizations. Overall, companies favour internal types of training (with possible outside assistance) because (a) they cost less; and (b) they are a more natural choice when training is in the requirements and techniques specific to the company.

   Large groups of employees will almost always be trained internally, often with internal and external training staff. Small groups and

Fig. 4.1 Continuous education – use of funds by companies

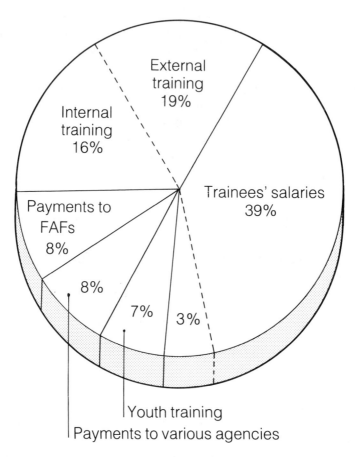

Source: Chamber de Commerce et d'Industrie de Paris, 1985

individuals are almost always trained externally, particularly for promotion purposes. Consequently, the higher the hierarchical position, the greater the likelihood the training will be external.

Long external programmes are not numerous but their effect on the volume of training is far from negligible. Large companies send managers on management development programmes for between five weeks and several months (full or part-time) to management schools and centres such as the CPA (*Centre de Perfectionnement aux Affaires* – run by the Paris

Fig. 4.2 Continuous education market shares

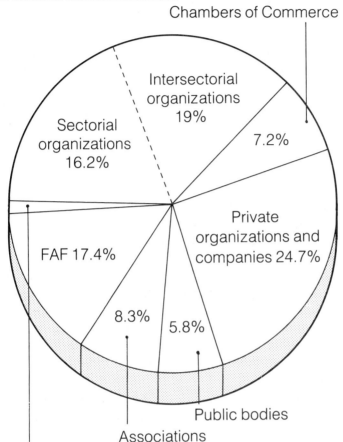

Chambers of Commerce

Intersectorial organizations 19%

Sectorial organizations 16.2%

7.2%

FAF 17.4%

Private organizations and companies 24.7%

8.3%

5.8%

Public bodies

Associations

1.4% Miscellaneous

Source: Cambre de Commerce et d'Industrie de Paris, 1985

Chamber of Commerce), ISSEC (the continuing education division of ESSEC), INSEAD and the IAEs (*Instituts d'Administration des Entreprises*, which are units within the university sector concentrating on doctoral and management programmes). These are usually paid for in full by companies but are often not included in the declared training budget nor mentioned in the *plan de formation*.

CPA, ISSEC, INSEAD and the IAEs offer a wide range of both specific and general management courses and are widely used for actual and potential senior managers. Prices in 1984 for these programmes ranged between 46 450 francs at CPA to 54 500 at INSEAD (excluding accommodation, travel, etc.). In many cases, to prevent poaching, companies require management staff to sign a contract committing them to stay with the company for a defined period. Because of the cost of these courses, few companies sponsor young managers on long MBA style courses (10 per cent sponsored at INSEAD and even less at ISA which is part of the HEC complex run by the Paris Chamber of Commerce). Most of these courses have extensive international links and participants can spend time in a European, American or Japanese business school. Foreign language teaching is a distinctive feature of many establishments both at graduate and continuing education level.

On the continuing education side, whilst there is a marked trend towards in-company courses, there is also a move on the part of large companies to stop using their own training centres (and their own trainers), in favour of using external resources (e.g.: of HEC and ISSEC). In all, there are over 6000 main training organizations, including the management centres, business schools, consultancies, etc., listed in an annual publication *Dicoguide de la formation*. A public central organization, INFFO, in Paris provides extensive information on training and training facilities and this is backed up by regional centres, called CARIF (*centres régionaux d'animation et de ressources de l'information sur la formation*). These are equipped with state-funded up-to-date computerized data banks allowing quick and accurate retrieval of information on all aspects and levels of training available, the French viewing such information as playing a key role in continuing education.

Young management development programmes are relatively rare, with the emphasis being on the acquisition of more specialist skills, a fact which again perhaps underlines the criticism that *grandes écoles* diploma studies are too generalist. Specialist courses abound, therefore, with a good number of companies spending over one third of their expenditure on computer-related training. Interpersonal skills (*communication* in French) come a close second, not just for managers but particularly for the supervisory grades at the sharp end of industrial relations. French companies are giving these *agents de maîtrise* increasing responsibility and placing more and more reliance on them to get across the commercial and economic realities of their business.

At the top end of the scale, very little management development is on offer for chairmen, managing directors, etc. On the whole, training managers enjoy little prestige in French companies and hence lack the muscle to effect such programmes, their prime concern being with junior and middle management levels.

Methods used

A wide variety exists, particularly on-the-job training which is widely used and believed by many to be the best there is, particularly for the young graduate theoreticians. One immediate problem, however, is that immediate superiors are seldom trained to train and there is an acute awareness of this as a major issue in France, with some companies, such as BSN, the largest food group, introducing 'cascade' systems of training. In conjunction with HEC and ESSEC, in BSN's marketing area, for example, managers are taught to lead seminars themselves and hence transfer their knowledge acquired from these schools, from the top downwards to all levels. It is not enough to have trained professional trainers, managers must increasingly assume this role. At Procter and Gamble, 60 per cent of a unit manager's job is training: 'If he doesn't train his people well, his business will suffer'. In EDF–GDF, they are keen to develop much further the idea of involving *cadres* in training. On-the-job training is an obvious area, but in decentralized training schemes, training is often undertaken by managers for two to three weeks annually and in the company's training centres, nearly all the trainers are managers who will return to their functions after three to four years.

External *à la carte* short courses are often seen as 'returning to school' and are criticized for being too passive and unrelated to company needs.

Open learning techniques are as yet undeveloped in France. Video training films are to be found in banks and insurance companies but computer assisted education, although arousing much interest, is, as yet, relatively little used. The UK seems a long way ahead in this respect, according to one observer.

Role of the plan de formation

The main objective of the training plan was to force companies to negotiate training matters with employees' representatives, usually the unions. It is intended to bring together in one document both corporate and individual objectives. The individual is often quoted as being the prime mover but generally needs are considered in the light of corporate needs. Through the means of annual assessments where these needs are expressed (and these vary in degrees of sophistication), there is intended to be a convergence of the two sides and general agreement on the content and timing of training. Some managers want more training, some do not and the amount of pressure exerted on them to do so varies considerably. In EDF–GDF, half of the managers went on training courses in 1985 and the company does not feel particularly proud of what it has done for the *cadres* in the last few years. Twenty years ago, the company was well in advance of other companies. This is no longer true, however, hence the determination to reinforce the quality of its management training. But there is no intention to go towards a system of obligatory training – training must be negotiated, albeit strongly advised.

In Pepro, an agro-chemical division of Rhône-Poulenc in Lyon, one of the top French chemical companies, out of 65 *cadres*, 53 received some form of training in 1986: training is seen as being an integral part of career development and is often the result of a very thorough individual assessment programme, which is monitored by computer and reminds managers monthly of their exact position on their schedule of assessments of subordinate managers. In the oil company, Total, a recent text sent by the chairman to all staff, underlines the importance of competence and stresses the duty of individuals to get themselves trained and of their superiors to make sure they do so.

The situation is very varied, then, oscillating between degrees of pressure and urgency displayed by some companies and a more benign, relaxed view, according to which the individuals must decide and take their future into their own hands. The position is also affected by two other factors. Firstly, how strong the trade unions are within a company and how far this strength is made to be felt in the *plan de formation*. And, secondly, the financial situation of the company. In the last few years, many French companies have had to face making drastic cuts in costs with the inevitable consequences for employment. In such circumstances, the training budget has been switched to retrain staff under the threat of redundancy and hence away from management training. The two factors are obviously linked, and a strong union presence could be decisive, to the benefit of the more unskilled grades.

Views on the importance of the training plan are conflicting. The larger the company, the more useful it is considered to be. To the smaller companies, it is an irksome bind. Observers in training organizations hold the view that often the plan is purely a collection of disparate needs, a mish-mash put together to comply with the legal obligation. The issue of a strategic policy over the next five years is rarely broached and training adds up to nothing more than a response to short-term requirements, e.g.: computerization. Often the whole question depends very much on the personality of the human resources manager and whether he can push a cohesive plan at board level. A very good example of a successful plan is to be found in SCREG, a company in the large, but, to graduates, unglamorous sector of the construction and civil engineering industry. Here, training is decided centrally by the chairman and managing director plus regional directors and four to five key head office staff. From September to December 1985, some 500 *cadres* worked, in commissions of ten, on future strategies, techniques, personnel and communications. The result was a training plan until March 1988 encompassing the major issues delineated by the commissions, e.g.: quality control and aimed at top management downwards. 'Our company is ambitious, we want to be number one and therefore training is for competence.'

Role of the 'congé individuel de formation'

Compared with the other legal provisions for training, the individual training leave is of recent creation (1982 and 1984) and was intended to resolve the dilemma caused by the conflict between corporate and individual needs. What the individual wanted was not always what the company wanted, pointing to a basic underlying assumption made by companies that all training has to be of benefit to them. Hence, the ultimate split occurred in the 1.2 per cent between the 0.8 per cent devoted to the training plan which would take account of corporate objectives and the 0.1 per cent earmarked for the individual. The training leave is considered as being of crucial relevance for the future, particularly for facilitating and hence increasing professional mobility. Any encouragement given to companies to see training as investment must have as its corollary, therefore, further provisions not only to enable the individual to acquire portable credentials but also to modernize the whole structure whereby this may be achieved. Some companies have gone so far as to treat the 1.2 per cent purely for the interests of employees: any further expenditure beyond the legal limit would then constitute the company's investment for its own purposes. Most have rejected this compartmentalization as being impossible to implement, particularly in times of financial constraint. Nor would it be very motivating for the work-force, particularly where demand exceeded the supply available under the 0.8 per cent limit.

Not much evidence was found that companies were making much use of the *congé individuel de formation*, or to be more precise, that individuals were being allowed to take advantage of its availability. One company official was adamant that it was unnecessary (it had received only five demands in ten years), since all requests for individual training were met without it. In another company, there was complete resistance even to advertising its availability too widely in case too many applied and hence jeopardized the smooth running of the company by their absence.

The widespread fear expressed was that, on obtaining a more portable credential, managers would leave. The system is a double-edged sword, however, and could well be increasingly seen as an important device to encourage voluntary redundancies in the present economic circumstances in France, in which there has been a marked rise in overdue shake-outs. Managers will increasingly use it to change companies – which might want them to go anyway.

Small and medium-sized companies (PME)

Generally speaking it is thought that school and continuing education are more rarely seen as resources in the PME than in the large companies, although the regional business schools supply a fair share of the PME top managers. The personality of candidates is of more interest than their qualifications in those PME where rigid and strictly codified hierarchies are less prevalent and good interpersonal relationships are important. In addition, the more qualified the employees on entry, the greater the likelihood they will leave, having more open access to the labour market. Considering the salary and status differences, it is scarcely surprising to find that there is a distinct shift towards large companies by employees with diplomas. This is occurring at a time when the majority of new jobs are being created in the PME and when, for managers, job opportunities in the PME are better than in any other sector, mainly because the original founders are of retiring age and seeking replacements. Time may be running out to grow their own managers and they may be compelled to take a chance on employing more formally qualified staff.

The views of the PME on the obligatory 1.2 per cent are very varied and often contradictory. Either it is seen as an added tax burden, or as a budget which they have to manage as best they can, or the amount levied has become ridiculously low. Most companies are agreed on the importance of training, however; their complaints are reserved for the system. The definition of what is allowed under the levy is too restrictive and administrative and gives preference to types of training which have little relevance to the PME. On the other hand, many companies, are unable to release personnel and attempt to cover their requirements, by internal practices and techniques which do not conform to the norm. 'In our job, training is not formalized. When there's a need we try to respond, with or without the 1.1 per cent, whether the training is allowable or not.' Costs incurred by on-the-job training cannot be included and this has the affect that many PME fail to reach the legal minimum. This means that the balance must be paid either to recognized training bodies or, as a last resort, the public Treasury. The feeling that a company is financing the training of someone else's staff does not go down too well in some small companies.

The declaration form 2483 is also the subject of some frustration, too, being yet one more constraint. In large companies it would be completed by the training department: in the PME, it is often compiled by someone totally unconnected with training policy, by an accountant, or even an external agency, for example. Its quantitative type of evaluation is seen as irrelevant and some companies would like to have it substituted by a more qualitative system they regularly use and which would then have the knock-on effect of encouraging other companies to reflect on the effectiveness of their own training practices.

The *plan de formation* is often not the result of the more sophisticated procedures used in the larger companies. Some companies, however, have initiated systems in which annual appraisals are used as the basis for determining needs which are then co-ordinated with corporate objectives. Issue-driven training is of growing importance and one example was found of a company in Paris employing some 140 staff where training was an integral part of a general company project involving all staff in stages, starting with the management and working down through the company to quality circles.

M. Le Gorrec at EDF–GDF sees no particularly promising trends on the horizon for the PME. Discussions are being held with the government in an attempt to explore ways of making more use of the levy to help the PME. There are no foolproof legal ways, however, and much depends on finding other solutions. Large companies are increasingly making their training centres available to their subcontractors, often the PME. At EDF-GDF, a replacement is supplied for staff being trained, thereby enabling companies to overcome one of the major handicaps they experience. Local initiatives are being encouraged: for example, in one *département*, Charente-Maritime, PMEs, large companies and training schools have pooled their resources in an attempt to invent new and original forms of training.

COMPARISONS WITH OTHER PROFESSIONS

It is still axiomatic that engineering schools represent the royal way to success, both in state service and private enterprise. The growing number of business schools are snapping hard at their heels, however, and have hitherto represented a serious threat to the engineers' supremacy, even in general management posts. In spite of moves through the *Junior-entreprises* to bring the two types of school together, rivalry is still intense. Business schools are gearing themselves up to introduce more technology into their curriculum (with one school in Grenoble working closely with a consortium of engineering schools in the area of industrial marketing). Engineering schools are hitting back by integrating more management studies into their course content. The newest development, however, is the number of senior managers (37 per cent in large companies) with a double diploma, one in engineering and another in management (French business school or an MBA).

In contrast, accountancy suffers from the same image as the medical profession: backward, out-of-date and requiring too long a period of study (i.e.: eight to nine years). In HEC, for example, auditing courses are attracting fewer and fewer participants. Numerically speaking, the profession is still small by British standards with some 10 000 practising chartered accountants, of whom 17 per cent are found in auditing firms and 83 per cent in industrial and service companies. Annual salaries are high, averaging some 500 000 francs. It is generally recognized that although positions in financial management are highly prized, there is a severe shortage of accountants. Finance could well be the new 'royal' way to general management, as in West Germany, where the top two in many companies are ex-finance directors.

Law and medical studies are organized in universities, there being no selection on entry, but a *numerus clausus* ensures a high drop-out at the end of the first year. Doctors and lawyers receive high salaries, although there is now a surplus of the former, a situation which has led in some areas to unemployment in the profession. An increasing tendency is for business schools such as HEC and ESSEC to allow more doctors and lawyers into the second year of their undergraduate courses.

COMMENTARY

Mention has already been made of the striking extent to which there has been a noticeable change in the attitude, not just of managers but the population as a whole towards industry. Until some four to five years ago, the world of the 'company' and of industry in general was the object of intellectual scorn, fanned by a pervasive current of left-wing anti-profit thought. Camus and Sartre were not obscure philosophers but wrote novels which were devoured by an eager populace. Their brand of social democracy in the belated industrialization period of the 1950s and 1960s led many to turn their back on the materialism they spawned. For the élite, it was more 'noble' to be *inspecteur des finances* or an engineer working in the Civil Service or a State corporation rather than the financial or technical director in a private company.

Following the two oil shocks of the 1970s, it was industry which paid the price, in terms of index-linked salaries and high social charges, for France's failure to appreciate that the days of constant and rapid growth were over and that the State could no longer be all-providing. The individual Frenchman and woman were cushioned against reality and continued to live a life of State-assisted comfort and ease. With the disastrous Socialist economic experiment of 1981–3 and the ultimate U-turn of the government, there has been a rapid loss of illusions, amidst bouts of tough straight talking. The reality of the situation is now accepted by all (the French still speak of a continuing crisis – *la crise*), and particularly the notion that companies produce wealth and therefore jobs. The Socialist government's endorsement of this view gave it even greater credence. The decline of the Communist party (from over 20 per cent of the national vote in 1981 to less than 10 per cent at present) and of the unions, and the latest fashion of liberalism and less State intervention have all been influential factors. It has become the norm to be interested in the economy, in stocks and shares, in the money markets. Business and economic publications have proliferated, underlining this new mood.

The repercussions for management could ultimately be far-reaching. Fewer of the élite are attracted by the security of the Civil Service and the lure of its automatic end-of-year bonuses and the light-green Renault 25. Even the highly prestigious Civil Service training school, the *École Nationale d'Administration* is halving its intake as the State itself plays a part by slimming down. Those who once preferred the enormous status of an *Eaux et Forêts* engineer (Forestry Commission and Water Board) in one of the regions are now turning to the dynamic sectors of the manufacturing and service industries, which are hence being supplied with more and more of the best academically qualified manpower of the country. Ten years ago, public administration courses were amongst the most popular at HEC, now entrepreneurship has taken over the number one spot. According to M. Vulliez, once Director of HEC and now head of the Paris Chamber of Commerce's education department, 'Company bosses enjoy more legitimacy in the public's eyes than politicians. And you can't go from the Civil Service into top companies unless you're worth your salt'.

The emphasis on diplomas has become more intense, but at the same time more attention is being paid to personal qualities, good leadership and communication skills and the ability to motivate. The emphasis is now and will increasingly be on 'professionalism', not just the possession of basic skills, but the competence to use these as a means to a professional end and to collective success. One indication of this is the growing acceptance of salary increases which are no longer automatic as in the past but based on merit.

Many believe that the academically educated managers, particularly those from the *grandes écoles*, lack this sort of professionalism. Managers need to know more than how to solve problems: they must also discern their existence and implement their solutions. As a result of this new emphasis on professionalism there is growing importance attached to training in interpersonal skills at all levels. This is accompanied by a move to bring training more within the ambience and control of the company ('We must demystify *formation initiale* and promote *formation continue*). Public, off-the-shelf courses are no longer so popular. In their place, more companies (e.g.: SCREG and BSN) and even some of the PME are organizing courses linked to the strategic issues and dilemmas of the company. External consultants, often from the business schools, are employed to help with the design and delivery of these courses, but for their success they depend on the commitment and involvement of senior management. Continuing education is by this means becoming more rooted in the organization than by any attempts by government to increase the obligation to train through statutory means.

Another aspect of the new emphasis on professionalism is the growing requirement for technical competence in specialist areas to counterbalance the tendency of the *grandes écoles* to provide too generalist a background. One indication of the importance attached to specialist knowledge is the popularity of the new *mastère* courses in a wide variety of both engineering and management skills. Abbreviated to an MS (an attempt perhaps to match the international attraction and credibility of an Anglo-Saxon MSc) these courses last one year and can be taken immediately after a graduate course or after years of experience. They are often sponsored and financed by groups of companies. A *mastère* in computers at ESSEC, for example, is financed by IBM and Borroughs.

Another area of growing importance is entrepreneurship. Company start-ups are increasing by 8 per cent per year. Courses in entrepreneurship, take-overs, and bankruptcy are popular. They provide a correction to the traditional criticism that the *grande école* education discourages risk-taking and initiatives. A *polytechnicien* is not supposed to make mistakes.

THE FUTURE

A government sponsored book *Où va la formation des cadres?* (Where is management development going?) recently identified issues facing managers in the future. They included:

● new organization models made possible or necessary by new technology;

- social pressures created by an increasingly well-qualified work-force demanding more autonomy and participation;
- an increasing number of women in managerial roles;
- a move towards more flexible models of organization which allow more personal initiative and the development of human potential;
- the need for better management of innovation and quality;
- the growing importance of the international dimension.

Organizations were spotlighted which are aware of the need and have developed relevant training packages and approaches. These include the Crédit Agricole, the Banque de France, ESSEC, the Technological University of Compiègne and several regional business schools.

The main concerns in many companies are directed at the effects of the growing levels of education and training on their older employees. More and better qualified young people coming out of the engineering schools and the universities are affecting the promotional chances of those who had joined earlier with a more lowly vocational qualification. Unless these latter are given the opportunity to earn promotion by more continuing education there might be social problems in some industries. This situation is already faced by EDF-GDF because of the turndown in the nuclear energy field and the switching of some of its more qualified work-force to the more conventional forms of electricity generation. The trend is going to be experienced more widely yet as companies who have traditionally promoted everyone in-house begin to hire in outside specialists to cope with unanticipated change and the need for new expertise. At the lower levels, with the increasing responsibilities and training given to the supervisory grades and technicians, there are fewer promotion opportunities for workers to come up from the ranks *autodidacte* as in the past. The need, therefore, for more continuing education specifically geared to portable professional credentials of some sort is great and is growing. Government planning organizations are aware of its implications and are urging both greater recourse to the individual training leave by employees and less fear by companies of its possible consequences. Only then will training be seen as requiring a comprehensive and cohesive organization, integrating initial training and both corporate needs and self-development as a right. 'Perhaps one of the biggest changes in the future will be the way people get their diploma. More will and must get it through continuing education.'

The dilemma faced by the education system is to do with the appropriateness of traditional French selection methods and education. It is felt by many that a system that takes mathematics as the most important single criterion for entrance to a business education shuts out much potential talent. More talent is increasingly needed and many would like to see more *grandes écoles* established to meet the demand, even at the expense of relenting a little on selection methods. The universities will still continue to provide a major headache to any government. They represent a vast reservoir of untapped resources, but there are few signs of better distribution and management of these resources within the university system, and most certainly not within an integrated university/*grandes écoles* system. As long as they are seen as second best and remain stigmatized by industry, they could continue to form a smouldering volcano of resentful energy.

'Any manager without overseas experience in five years time will be seriously handicapped.' This is an opinion proffered at time when French industry has become very rapidly international both in outlook and structure. They are aware of these trends in the business schools, however, and laudable efforts are being made to internationalize their activities, through work assignments and links with other schools abroad. Most place great stress on the importance of the European market and are well aware of the implications of the single European market promised for 1992.

Finally, there is the challenge posed to French firms by the growing number of women entering management. In most business schools women now represent 40 per cent to 50 per cent of the intake and 18.2 per cent of the students at engineering schools. Yet only 1 per cent of managing directors, and 4 per cent of senior managers are women. Overall, some 20 per cent of *cadres* are women, with some 90 per cent of these being in the service sector. These numbers might change, but only slowly. Given the very large number of higher education students going through business schools, the increasing feminization of the schools will hardly dent the management labour market. The numbers may well change, however, particularly in the ranks of middle management supplied by the universities and other means. The Roudy Act of July 1983 provides for better information being collected within companies to allow them to have a better appreciation of the place and role of women in their organizations. Time will tell whether such an appreciation will lead to better job promotion and training prospects for women. This is already happening in a company like Moulinex which has a policy of positive discrimination in favour of recruiting more women for management positions. Perhaps the most important influence will be a progressive feminization of society with more dual careers and role-sharing and, as a result, a change in values. A recent report suggests that such a change has a long way to go. How all of this will affect the task of management and the formation of managers is not at all clear except that it adds yet more force to the view that the ways of the past will not be the only ways of the future.

5 WEST GERMANY

BY COLLIN RANDLESOME

INTRODUCTION

In a country where the 'rule of order and the law' (*Rechtsstaat*) is constantly emphasized, where the citizens pride themselves on being members of a 'high-performance society' (*Leistungsgesellschaft*), and where many are relishing the fruits of an 'affluent society' (*Wohlstandsgesellschaft*), it appears curious that nobody has taken the trouble to produce a legal definition of the occupation which is so readily associated with these three oustanding features of West Germany today – that of the 'manager' (*Führungskraft*)[1]. It follows, then, that if the term is not legally defined, there can be no official statistics on the number or type of managers actually operating in the country, and surveys or polls have to be relied upon.

Individual companies in West Germany are, however, in no doubt as to which of their employees 'manage' or 'lead' (*führen*) and which do not. Though designations of 'manager' vary, depending on company size and the sector of the economy in which the firm is involved, 'management' (*Führung*) can begin at the level of the master craftsman (*Meister*) or even the one below, i.e. that of the skilled worker (*Facharbeiter*). It culminates at management board level in public limited companies (*Aktiengesellschaften*) or managing directors' level in private limited companies (*Gesellschaften mit beschränkter Haftung*). How many levels of management come in between is, again, a function of the size of the company and the line of business in which it is engaged.

GERMAN THOUGHT AND EDUCATION

The education, training and development of managers in West Germany are a reflection of the German view of the world (*Weltanschauung*) and the educational ideals of Wilhelm von Humboldt.

Whereas man's achievements are classified in English-speaking countries according to the arts and the sciences, the Germans adopt a fundamentally different approach. They distinguish between the performing and fine arts (*Kunst*), all knowledge, science and some of the arts (*Wissenschaft*), and the fashioning of useful artefacts (*Technik*)[2]. The advertising slogan of the Audi car company, *Vorsprung durch Technik* ('In the lead through engineering') is not idly chosen because the word *Technik* is imbued with so many and varied connotations for the German mind.

The position of *Technik* as a category of man's accomplishments in its own right contrasts vividly with that of engineering in Anglo-Saxon countries. Here engineering stands as merely one of the applied sciences, which are in themselves a sub-category of science: in West Germany, *Technik* is pre-eminent because it embraces both the art and the science of making or manufacturing things.

This difference in thinking has significant implications for the West German economy and for the set of values cherished by the citizenry of the country. The pre-eminence of *Technik* gives rise to a manufacturing-friendly environment, with the result that West Germany has not moved too far towards a service economy. Over 30 per cent of gross domestic product is still furnished by manufacturing industry, where higher value is usually added than by services.

Techniker, one of the derivations of *Technik*, which means 'technician', possesses mainly positive overtones in the German language. To say of someone, '*Er ist ein guter Techniker*' would be to pay him the most sincere of compliments. In English, however, one might perhaps expect to encounter 'technician' used in a pejorative sense such as, 'He's a good technician all right, but . . .'[3]

The admiration of the *Techniker* reflects in West Germany a pervasive preference for the professional, by contrast with the British adoration of the amateur. The cult and cultivation of the professional, the expert, the *Techniker*, are thus the dominant features of higher education in West Germany. These same considerations also dominate the education of managers.

Much of today's education system in West Germany still aspires to the ideals of Wilhelm von Humboldt, 1767–1835, though some modern developments could not have been foreseen by him. A friend of Goethe and Schiller, von Humboldt was a man of actions rather than words. As a minister in the Prussian government, he founded the new University of Berlin, which was inaugurated in 1810. Von Humboldt laid the basis for the higher education of the nation by his practical realization of the ideas of Germany's classical poets and thinkers[4].

University education was perceived by von Humboldt as learning which should be based on a sound general education and which should advance 'in unity and freedom'. Both ideals live on today. The first, that of a sound general education, is reflected in the breadth of the curriculum for the examination leading up to university entrance, which is called *Abitur* or *Hochschulreife*. Here pupils of nineteen or twenty years of age must study, and be examined in, a wide range of subjects and not merely those which they intend to pursue at university. The second of von Humboldt's ideals, i.e. that studies should proceed 'in unity and freedom', finds its echo in the length of time which West German students spend at their universities. In these ancient establishments, with long academic traditions, especially in the promotion of rigorous thinking and scientific research, the average length of diploma studies is approximately 6.0 years for students of the economic sciences, 6.2 years for electrical and 6.4 for mechanical engineers[5]. The average cost of the courses to the students, of whom none receive grants and only one quarter loans, was in 1986 DM 61 000 for economic scientists, DM 66 100 for electrical engineers and DM 67 600 for mechanical engineers[6].

What von Humboldt could not have anticipated are the large numbers of students currently entering institutions of higher education in West Germany. From 79 400 young people starting their studies in 1960 and 125 700 in 1970, the figure reached 225 100 in 1982, representing 21.3 per cent of the average age group between 19 and 21. The number of student places increased not only as a result of larger age cohorts but also because of greater participation rates. Currently, some 75 per cent of those qualified to enter institutions of higher education do so[7].

Bringing together now the main strands of German thought and philosophies of education, what we witness today in tertiary education are vocationally-oriented, broadly-based and lengthy studies for large numbers of young people in West Germany, including future managers.

Fig. 5.1 Basic structure of the education system in West Germany

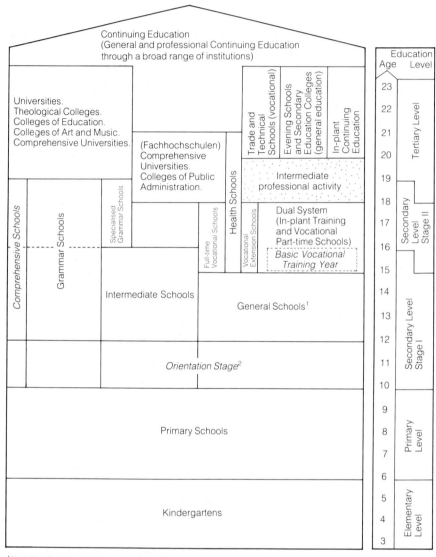

Continuing Education
(General and professional Continuing Education
through a broad range of institutions)

Universities.
Theological Colleges.
Colleges of Education.
Colleges of Art and Music.
Comprehensive Universities.

(Fachhochschulen)
Comprehensive
Universities.
Colleges of Public
Administration.

Trade and Technical Schools (vocational)

Evening Schools and Secondary Education Colleges (general education)

In-plant Continuing Education

Intermediate professional activity

Dual System
(In-plant Training
and Vocational
Part-time Schools)

Basic Vocational Training Year

Health Schools

Comprehensive Schools

Grammar Schools

Specialised Grammar Schools

Full-time Vocational Schools

Vocational Extension Schools

Intermediate Schools

General Schools[1]

Orientation Stage[2]

Primary Schools

Kindergartens

Education

Age Level

23
22
21
20   Tertiary Level
19
18   Secondary Level Stage II
17
16
15
14
13   Secondary Level Stage I
12
11
10
9
8   Primary Level
7
6
5
4   Elementary Level
3

[1]About 27 per cent of pupils in General Schools in addition attended an additional tenth school year.

[2]About 72 per cent of pupils in fifth and sixth school years attended the Orientation Stage.

*There are slight differences within the individual Länder

Figures in the right-hand column show the earliest possible age of entry in an uninterrupted progress through the education system.

The size of the rectangles is not proportional to the numbers attending.

Source: Grund- und Strukturdaten 1984/5: Der Bundesminister für Bildung und Wissenschaft

EDUCATION OF ASPIRING MANAGERS

A knowledge of the West German education system is essential to any understanding of how the country grows her managers because so much of the tradition begins in the schools, polytechnics and universities.

Future managers enter West German companies at any one of six different levels after experiencing types of education which vary greatly in duration and content (see also Fig. 5.1).

The lowest level of company entry, and one which is becoming increasingly rare as firms are able to be more selective in their recruitment policies, occurs after general school (*Hauptschule*) at the age of fifteen. Approximately 36 per cent of age group attend this type of school[8]. Award of the general school leaving certificate (*Hauptschulabschluß*) – the approximate equivalent of 5 CSE passes[9] – opens the way to many occupations for which formal training is required.

From here the route to management would lead via the status of apprentice (*Lehrling*), skilled worker (*Facharbeiter*) and master craftsman (*Meister*), with a parallel route open to to young people opting for a commercial apprenticeship (*kaufmännische Lehre*). Although one third of the senior managers at Daimler-Benz came up through the ranks, via the three year apprenticeship system, this is extremely rare in view of the increasing academization of management today – a trend which will be commented upon later (see pp. 134–137).

Company entry at the second level is feasible after attendance at an intermediate school (*Realschule*), at the age of sixteen. Approximately 28 per cent of age group attend this type of school, after selective entry[10]. Successful completion of the intermediate school leads to the award of the intermediate certificate (*Realschulabschluß* or *Mittlerer Abschluß*) – the rough equivalent of 5 O-level passes[11]. Possession of this certificate substantially improves a young person's chances of employment and with it the all-important apprenticeship in the dual system of work and part-time study. It also qualifies young people for attendance at a technical school (*Fachschule* or *Fachoberschule*), specialized schools offering vocational training at upper secondary level.

The third level of company entry can be achieved after completion of grammar school (*Gymnasium*) or of the upper technical and vocational school (*Fachoberschule*), at the age of nineteen or twenty. Approximately 26 per cent of age group attend grammar school, again after selective entry[12]. The final leaving certificate, *Abitur* or *Hochschulreife*, – the approximate but much broader-based equivalent of A-level – affords legal right of entry to universities or polytechnics (*Fachhochschulen*), subject to the number of places available in certain university faculties which operate a *numerus clausus*. Approximately 28 per cent of all pupils obtain this certificate or one of its close equivalents[13].

One equivalent, the *Fachhochschulreife*, is awarded for the most part by the upper technical and vocational schools (*Fachoberschulen*) and permits entry to polytechnics (*Fachhochschulen*), some of which also insist on admissions tests and/or interviews for certain subject areas, including 'business economics' (*Betriebswirtschaft*). The upper technical and vocational schools can also award the *Fachabitur*, a certificate which provides admission to a limited number of subjects at university.

A growing number of young people possessing the *Abitur* or one of its equivalents are opting not to go on to higher education, or at least not straight after school. Some 15 per cent of successful *Abitur* candidates elect to serve an apprenticeship first and then proceed to study at university[14]. This is not uncommon, for example, in banking, where 33 per cent of the trainee intake of the Bayerische Vereinsbank take this particular route.

Other successful candidates with *Abitur* choose special training courses (*Sonderausbildungsgänge für Abiturienten*), which are also enjoying growing popularity. These special courses differ from the traditional apprenticeship in both content, i.e. more theory has to be learned, and duration. They last in excess of three years. The number of companies offering such courses rose from 200 in 1977 to 800 in 1981, and the number of places available from 4000 to 6000. Eighty per cent of the places are for commercial assistants, 15 per cent for mathematical or technical assistants, and 5 per cent for engineering assistants. In 1981, there were 14 applicants for every place offered[15].

One of the reasons for the growing reluctance of young people to enter higher education at all, or at least not immediately after completing their secondary education, is to be found in graduate unemployment in West Germany – a theme which will be taken up later (see pp 154–156).

At this point it should be noted that West German males are obliged to perform national service, which used to last for 15 months but has recently been extended to 18 months.

The fourth level of company entry is after graduation from a polytechnic (*Fachhochschule*).

Most of the 118 polytechnics were set up in the early 1960s and developed from engineering schools (*Ingenieurschulen*), senior technical colleges (*Höhere Fachschulen*) for commerce (*Wirtschaft*), social studies (*Sozialwesen*), textiles and clothing (*Textilwirtschaft*).

There are several reasons why the individual federal states (*Bundesländer*), each of which enjoys great autonomy in matters of education and culture, were determined to promote the expansion of higher education outside the university sector:

- Polytechnic courses were to be of much shorter duration than university courses in similar disciplines, i.e. a maximum of three to four years;
- Polytechnic courses, particularly in 'business economics' (*Betriebswirtschaft*), were to be more practice-oriented than their theory-laden equivalents in the universities;
- Polytechnic courses were supposed to address more directly the regional demand for places of study as well as provide a supply of graduates commensurate with the needs of industry and commerce in the region[16].

There are approximately a quarter of a million students at polytechnics, with 1 per cent per annum more young people with the *Abitur* qualification electing to attend a polytechnic in preference to a university. This increasing percentage could become significant in future years when the number of young people entitled to study will begin to fall dramatically as from 1988[17], owing to West Germany's decline in birthrate, which has reached world-record proportions of only 1.4 children per woman.

The main subject areas, in order of popularity, studied at polytechnics are: mechanical and production engineering; economics and business economics; social studies; electrical engineering; public administration; architecture; civil engineering[18].

Most polytechnic courses are divided into: a foundation course (*Grundstudium*), which lasts for two years, and after which an examination must be taken; and a main studies section (*Hauptstudium*) lasting usually one year and requiring a diploma thesis as well as written and oral examinations.

In a large number of polytechnic courses, students are obliged to spend placement periods in industry or commerce (*Praxissemester*) during which they gain practical experience in their field of study.

A significant feature of some polytechnics, in terms of international management education, is to be found in a number of European business studies courses. These usually last for four years and always include periods of study in the UK and/or France. Often they also involve placement periods in industry or commerce abroad, and graduates receive double degrees. These graduates are much sought after by German companies, with approximately two-thirds of the students in the final year of the Reutlingen EBS programme receiving job offers before taking their final diploma. Schloß Reichartshausen am Rhein, a private polytechnic, has an equally proud placement record for its graduates[19]. The particular successes of these two programmes, however, serve to highlight a general failure by West Germany to provide an adequate supply of international managers – another theme to which subsequent reference will be made (see pp. 159–162).

To distinguish polytechnic qualifications from university qualifications in similar fields, some federal states insist that their polytechnics confer academic awards such as *Diplom-Ingenieur (FH)* or *Diplom-Betriebswirt (FH)*, the abbreviation in brackets referring to *Fachhochschule*.

The average age on graduation from a polytechnic is 26 years.

The fifth level of company entry is feasible after graduation from university at diploma standard.

Universities in West Germany differ from polytechnics in several ways. Firstly, they are on average much more ancient seats of learning with strong academic traditions, vigorously pursuing von Humboldt's ideals. Secondly, staff at universities tend to be better qualified academically than their polytechnic counterparts, but the latter have more practice-related experience. Thirdly, university faculties must teach and research: polytechnic faculties must teach and are entitled to research but this is not an obligation imposed upon them. Finally, as already mentioned, university courses are of greater duration than polytechnic courses. The average length of diploma studies for university graduates is 6.5 years. Though a longer period of study does not in itself imply a higher standard in the final diploma, there is a general consensus that the university award is higher than that from a polytechnic. This is also reflected in the fact that a polytechnic diploma entitles the holder to entry into the middle ranks of the West German civil service (*gehobener Dienst*); a university diploma to the higher ranks (*höherer Dienst*).

There are approximately 975 000[20] students attending universities in West Germany, including the comprehensive universities (*Gesamthochschulen*). Considering in addition to these the students at colleges of theology, art, music, education, and the polytechnics, it can be stated that approximately 20 per cent of the 19 to 25-year-olds in the country are enjoying the benefits of higher education.

The most popular courses at university are, in order of preference: the economic sciences, including business economics; law; medicine; German; education; mechanical and production engineering; politics and social sciences[21].

University graduates in general, and business economics graduates in particular, have been the subject of criticism on the grounds that their learning is too theoretical in nature. Possibly their most vociferous critic was Hans Dichgans, a businessman and delegate to the Federal Parliament (*Bundestag*), who had a public exchange of views on the subject with some twenty university professors of business economics in the 1960s[22]. According to Dichgans and many others, there is a marked lack of adequate practice-related teaching in university courses. Ironically enough, polytechnic graduates have recently been finding it increasingly difficult to escape similar criticism since the stipulation was dropped for them to serve an apprenticeship prior to polytechnic entry.

The consensus among companies would appear to be that university graduates are good abstract thinkers but require a two-year 'apprenticeship' in the business before they are really useful. Polytechnic graduates possess much more practical experience on entry and as a consequence are up and running from the very beginning of their company careers. This may well be why so large a percentage of polytechnic graduates find employment in medium-sized and small companies, where induction training is rare.

The average age of university students on graduation at diploma standard is 28 years.

The sixth and final level of company entry occurs after completion of doctoral studies at university.

In 1960, the total number of doctorates awarded by the West German universities was 6200: in the 1980s, approximately 13 000 students per annum graduate with the coveted doctor title, among whom there are some 2600 mathematics and social science graduates, 1300 economic and social scientists, and 1000 engineers[23].

The doctor title is almost essential for the upper ranks of management of certain companies, for example in the chemical industry or in insurance. In other branches of industry and commerce, the pay-off rate of the title is very difficult to quantify. The doctorate in economics or business economics is rewarded much more highly than the diploma in certain staff and line positions, though here, too, a young person with the title might be circumspect about accepting a post such as Assistant to Member of the Board – 'glorified secretary with a doctor title'. Moreover, a doctorate can be a positive hindrance for inclusion on some trainee programmes[24].

It cannot be denied, however, that the doctor title is a great help in promotion in industry and commerce: of the top managers in large companies who have studied one of the economic sciences at university, approximately two-thirds possess the doctorate[25].

The average age on graduation with the doctor title is 30 years.

ACADEMIZATION OF MANAGEMENT

Having identified the six levels of company entry and having commented on the type of education enjoyed by the aspiring managers coming in at the various levels, it is now possible to appreciate the significance of the bar chart (see Fig.5.2):

- The figure for West German managers holding a diploma at the managing director level was 62 per cent in 1984; in 1974, it was 58 per cent.
- The figure for managers holding a diploma at the 'first' level of management was 55 per cent in 1984; in 1974, it was 36 per cent.
- The figure for managers holding a diploma at the 'second' level of management was 44 per cent in 1984; in 1974, it was 28 per cent[26].
- The higher the position in the company hierarchy, the greater the number of graduates.

But the academization of management does not stop at the diploma level (see Fig. 5.3).

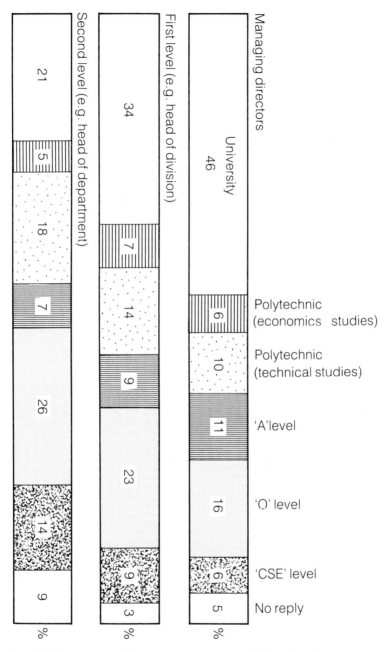

Fig. 5.2. Educational qualifications of managers in the Federal Republic of Germany
Sources: Institut der deutschen Wirtschaft, 1985 and Kienbaum Vergütungsberatung, 1984

Fig. 5.3 Educational qualifications of management board members of the 100 largest German companies

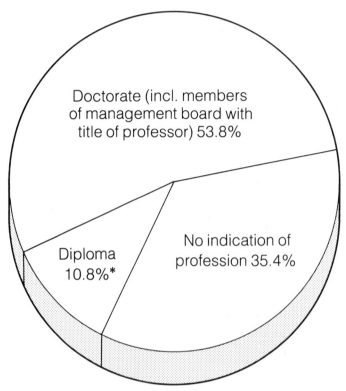

Doctorate (incl. members of management board with title of professor) 53.8%

Diploma 10.8%*

No indication of profession 35.4%

*Includes 5.4% engineers and 4.5% economic scientists

Source: Dr Frank Grütz Unternehmensberatung, Bergisch Gladbach

- In the 100 largest West German Public Limited Companies (AGs), some 53.8 per cent of management board members possess the doctorate. At Siemens, 14 of the 20 members of this board have the doctor title; at Bayer and the Deutsche Bank, 10 of the 12 members of this board are entitled to be addressed as 'Herr Doktor'.
- Taking the West German AGs quoted on the stock exchange, the figure for management board members with the doctorate is 41.5 per cent.

- In all West German AGs, 36.7 per cent of management board members sport the doctor title.
- The number of managers with doctorates is highest in the chemical industry, at 1371, if 'manager' is defined as managing director, member of the board of management, member of the board of supervisors or 'procurist'; second position is held by the machinery-manufacturing sector, with 859 doctorates; third by insurance, with 729 doctorates.
- The picture is similar if the average number of managers with doctorates per company is examined. Here insurance companies lead with an average of 2.13 doctors per company; second place is held by chemical firms, with 1.46. Bringing up the rear are building companies, with 0.13. The average number of managers with doctorates per company is 0.44, provided the term 'manager' is defined as above[27].
- The percentage of doctors in 'management' is greater:
- the larger the company;
- the higher the overall percentage of graduates in the firm;
- the more technologically-based the branch of industry.

THE MBA

At this point it would appear appropriate to pose the question: why did West Germany not see fit to establish American-style business schools, public or private, attached to existing universities or not, and awarding MBA degrees when other European countries were doing so in the 1960s?*

Firstly, at this particular time, West Germany was still enjoying unprecedented economic prosperity as a result of the Economic Miracle (*Wirtschaftswunder*), so why change a successful formula? Secondly, there were no initiatives forthcoming from the ministries of education in the individual federal states, where ex-professors, brought up in the German tradition, are the decision-makers. Thirdly, Germany has a long tradition in teaching and research in business economics, with the first college of commerce (*Handelshochschule*) being founded in Leipzig in 1898, and many of the first and best economics journals being published in Germany[28].

* A certain attempt was made at the *Universitätsseminar der Wirtschaft* (USW) but it foundered, *inter alia*, on the inappropriateness of American case studies to the West German business environment and business systems in general.

Moreover, these days business economics curricula are not dissimilar from MBA curricula. Finally, if polytechnic students graduate with an average age of 26, university students at diploma level at 28, and at the doctorate level at 30; and if the MBA degree is to be a post-experience qualification, at what age would a West German MBA student even start his or her studies?

So, a citizen of the country would have to go abroad to acquire an MBA. In 1985, there was not a single West German on the Harvard MBA programme; there were two at Stanford and two at Wharton[29]. Moreover, West Germans account for only 4 per cent of participants on the INSEAD programme[30].

This apparent lack of enthusiasm for the MBA qualification must conceal particular attitudes to it within the country, which prove to be ambivalent. In interviews conducted in a sample of West German companies, reactions to MBA graduates ranged from the sarcastic ('Ah, you mean these so-called international infant prodigies') to the adulatory ('Employing MBAs in this company would be tantamount to casting pearls before swine').

A more measured view is evident in large, West German companies which actually employ MBA graduates. Yet here, too, reactions are mixed. MBAs are praised above all for their analytical skills, their ability to work together in international teams, and their aggressiveness. When compared to the products of the West German polytechnics and universities, they are often referred to as 'pike in a carp-pond.' They are, however, criticized for what are perceived as their exaggerated initial salary expectations, and the suspicion lingers among personnel managers that their insistence on such is due to the thoroughly unwholesome influence of university placements officers abroad. Since neither MBAs nor university placements officers* are 'made in West Germany', this criticism may be accounted for by the Not-Invented-Here Syndrome.

MBA graduates are virtually unknown in medium-sized and small companies. They are, however, much sought after by firms of management consultants, many of whom ruthlessly exploit the MBA qualifications of their employees in the publicity which they target at the larger companies.

* University professors in West Germany often act as clearing-houses for the placement of their students. They maintain informal links with companies, and certain graduates are 'recommended' to firms for consideration.

RECRUITMENT CRITERIA FOR
FUTURE MANAGERS

In keeping with the tradition of the *Techniker* and the passion for the professional, West German companies perceive the management task in strictly functional terms, especially for middle and lower managers. Hence the direct relationship between vocational training or studies and the job to be done is of the utmost significance.

The importance of appropriate, vocationally-relevant diploma studies to the profession envisaged can perhaps be deduced from a survey conducted into the employment of humanities graduates in the Hamburg area in 1980. Fifty-nine companies, each with in excess of 1000 employees on payroll, were contacted for information about their humanities graduates. Forty-nine companies (83 per cent) responded, only 7 of which had such graduates on their staff. A grand total of 13 humanities graduates were found to be employed in the 49 companies[31].

What, then, are West German companies looking for when they seek to recruit university or polytechnic graduates? There are a number of factors which can be found to be for or against an applicant.

The particular university at which a young person chooses to study is not regarded as important by company recruiters unless one of the more problematical, left-wing universities has been attended, in particular Bremen and the Free University of Berlin. Nor are the differences between universities and comprehensive universities held to be significant. However, graduation from a highly-reputed economics faculty such as Cologne, Bonn or Mannheim can be an advantage when applying for a first job, since some heads of personnel departments have a long acquaintance with the products of these institutions.

Equally, the examination mark at diploma level must be judged in connection with the faculty or the professor involved. Companies are under no illusions about which faculties and which professors demand higher examination standards than others. A mark of 4 on the traditional scale of 1 to 6, where 1 is the highest mark, would tend to disqualify an applicant from consideration by most companies. If a very specialized position in the company is to be filled, a high mark in the appropriate subject can, however, offset a lower cumulative average.

Quite apart from any benefits it might bestow during the study period itself, a traditional apprenticeship, or a higher vocational qualification, is particularly esteemed by West German companies. This is especially true of small or medium-sized firms. Periods of practical experience during studies, in West Germany or preferably abroad, are also highly regarded by recruiting companies.

The diploma thesis written just before the final examination can be of importance, but this depends on whether it is a freely-chosen, scientific piece of work or something less weighty which has been polished off in six or eight weeks. If a topic has been thoroughly researched in all its theoretical and practical implications, and if it is linked to the position in the company being sought, then a good diploma thesis can be of value.

University studies which have been completed in four to four and a half years are not necessarily deemed by heads of personnel departments to be proof of excellence in an applicant. Complaints are sometimes voiced that such young people of, say, 25 years of age, lack the required maturity. Alternatively, someone who has studied for more than seven years would have to articulate some very convincing reasons for his or her dilatoriness. The best recruitment chances are enjoyed by those who have completed their studies in five to five and a half years. Thus the ideal age for a male applying for his first job would be between 26 and 28 years, with national service and possibly an apprenticeship behind him. Female university graduates would be one and a half to two years younger because they have not performed national service. It should also be noted that a maximum age of between 28 and 30 years is stipulated for participation in most graduate trainee programmes.

A second course of studies (Zusatzstudium) can also be useful when applying for a job. Graduates in business economics aiming to enter insurance or banking might be advised to take a doctorate in law.

Some polytechnic graduates have better initial chances of recruitment than their university counterparts, particularly those specializing in marketing or data processing. If, however, a polytechnic graduate wishes to enter one of the classic functional areas of a company, such as internal auditing or corporate planning, he or she would have better employment chances after moving on to a university and taking an additional course there[32].

All West German companies interviewed were at pains to stress that it is not only the qualifications but also the personality of the applicant that are the major determinants in the decision to appoint or not to appoint. A further, frequently-voiced comment was, 'Naturally, we want the best; but we need Indians as well as chiefs'.

POST-ENTRY INDUCTION TRAINING

The great majority of university and polytechnic graduates do not undergo any specific induction training on entry into companies. They have been cultivated in the *Techniker* mould, so their higher education has been work-related. They enter an area of functional management within a company and begin to function, but *not* to manage. If, in the fullness of time, they aspire to the status of manager, they would be advised not merely to function but to perform in contemporary West Germany's high-performance society.

Graduate entrants to large companies are treated in one of three ways. Some, like their counterparts in small and medium-sized companies, receive nothing other than on-the-job experience. 'They are thrown into the freezing water and told to swim – it's ridiculous.'

Others are exposed to on-the-job training in addition to job rotation – but only in a limited number of departments, say two or three at most. They might also receive an occasional course run within the company but they would hardly ever be sent on an external course at this tender age! Even participation in internal courses is not axiomatic because often the initiative for such is left to the individual concerned. 'There is a lot on offer in this company, and one thing we do expect of our young employees is the ability to put up their hand and ask.'

A very small minority of graduates entering large companies in the manufacturing sector (chemical, computer, food-processing, and car companies) or in the service sector (insurance and banking) do receive the opportunity to participate in a graduate trainee programme[33]. Normally, the numbers on these programmes are low, at less than 5 per cent of graduate intake. Participants in such programmes are highly qualified, totally mobile, and fluent in at least two foreign languages.

The length of the trainee programmes varies from sector to sector: in manufacturing it tends to be one year to eighteen months; in services two or more years.

The content of the programmes comprises on-the-job training, job rotation in several departments, and regular internal courses. In the most unlikely event of an external course being attended, it will be one of the closed-company type that has been carefully selected and tailored to the particular needs of the firm.

Graduate trainees in West German companies are not regarded as 'high-flyers' or 'fast-trackers', only as 'high-potentials'. They still have to prove to the company that they can perform. The Daimler-Benz attitude is typical of all the large West German companies interviewed: 'The better they are educated, the higher the track, but not necessarily the faster the track. It's not the education or the training that decides on a career in this company, it's the performance and nothing but the performance'.

MANAGEMENT DEVELOPMENT

As with the induction training of future managers, a distinction must be made in the development of managers between large, medium-sized and small companies. Many large companies have set up extensive management development programmes which are provided for internally. Some medium-sized firms display a marked awareness of the need to develop their managers but, because they do not possess the resources, they are obliged to send their managers on external courses. Most small companies claim that they have neither the time nor the money to indulge in any management development.

In West German companies, the initiative for management development lies with the individual concerned, his or her immediate superior, and perhaps the head of department or head of division. The personnel and training departments have only an indirect bearing on proceedings. This relationship reflects the prevailing philosophy of virtually all West German companies that the influence of the line must always be stronger than that of staff departments. In most companies, managers and their subordinates are subject to reviews either annually or biennially. Not only performance assessments but also development needs are discussed on these occasions between the manager, his superior and possibly head of department or division. In some firms, the reviews are accompanied by career forecasts covering the next five years.

If the individual employee is fortunate enough to have an enlightened superior, then he or she can be reasonably confident that development needs will be met. If this is not the case, then the individual has little recourse to any other point in the company. Theoretically, anyone feeling that their development needs are not being accommodated could approach the personnel department but they would be extremely reluctant to do so.

The prevailing view in West German companies is that superiors must have full sovereignty over their staff because it is the superior who is ultimately responsible for meeting departmental or divisional financial targets. It is only on the occasion of the superior's own annual or biennial review, at which a member of the personnel department might be present, that lack of sympathy for the management development of subordinates, and with it a certain neglect of corporate aims as opposed to departmental or divisional targets, could be brought to the superior's attention.

In large companies, the pattern is for lower management to receive more development than middle management, who in turn receive more than senior management. In these companies, 90 to 95 per cent of management development is performed internally, either by company trainers, senior managers in the company, or bought-in specialists from universities or polytechnics. When external staff are employed on internal courses, their contributions are thoroughly vetted before the course begins.

Large West German companies state that their reasons for organizing management development internally are firstly that they can do the job more effectively than anyone else. Secondly, they have the development resources, human, physical and financial, so they are determined to use them. Thirdly, they perceive internal courses, run at their own fabulously-located and equipped development centres, to be a means of inculcating their specific corporate culture and thus stimulating the employee to identify with this culture.

The content of the internal courses varies in accordance with the level of management involved. For lower management, the courses are inevitably of a technical nature and are often classified as *Fortbildung*, i.e. 'upgrading', or an extension of initial vocational training (*Ausbildung*). Examples in the manufacturing sector are courses on quality assurance or safety at work.

Above and beyond the level of *Fortbildung* is what would be understood in Anglo-Saxon countries as more specific management development (*Weiterbildung*), which normally begins at the level of middle management. Typical examples of internally-run courses for middle managers would include: the selection, assessment and promotion of staff; problem-solving and decision-making; and conflict management.

Courses attended by senior management cover such topics as time management; presentation skills; and the company and the environment. The latter courses are now often obligatory for senior managers because the recent successes of 'The Greens', the West German ecological party, have brought about a heightened consciousness of the company and its environment. This concern embraces environment in all its aspects within the country – physical, social, economic and political.

Internally-run foreign language courses are accessible to all levels of management on a need-to-know basis.

The 5 to 10 per cent of management development pursued by large companies in the form of external courses involves senior and, to a lesser extent, middle management, apart from the few highly-specialized programmes required by lower management.

One of the perquisites of top management can be attendance at the Baden-Baden entrepreneurs' colloquia (*Baden-Badener Unternehmergespräche*), which last for three weeks and are open to representatives from many firms. At these colloquia, subjects of common and topical interest to entrepreneurs and top managers are discussed, for example the security of managers. It must not be forgotten that Hanns-Martin Schleyer, one of West Germany's foremost businessmen, was kidnapped and executed by the 'Red Army Faction' (RAF). More recently, Karl Heinz Beckurts, director of research at Siemens, was blown up by a terrorist bomb.

The Baden-Baden colloquia have been running since 1954, and the average age of participants is 46 years[34]. Of the 2206 participants in the colloquia from 1954 to 1984, only 9 were female. Eight of the 9 women were entrepreneurs.

An institution providing external courses for senior and middle managers, predominantly from large companies, is the *Universitätsseminar der Wirtschaft* (USW) at Erfstadt/Liblar. Situated in a moated castle, this is not a university but a short course centre. Here 55 per cent of the courses are of the single-company or closed variety, where the main demand is for marketing programmes, corporate planning and the soft skills.

There appears to be a marked reluctance among large West German companies to send their staff on external courses which are open to a number of companies. When questioned about this tendency, one head of management development replied, 'Well, one of our suppliers might be attending the same course or, God forbid, one of our customers. This would put us in an intolerable position'.

Nonetheless, the USW does run a six-week general management

programme which is open to participants from a number of companies. The average age of participants on all USW courses is 40 years. Attendance by women is less than 1 per cent. Quite clearly, then, the position of women in management in West Germany is a theme to which subsequent reference will have to be made (see pp. 149–152).

Only a handful of the 68 universities in West Germany offer management development programmes, and even the terminology chosen to characterize the courses, *Kontaktseminare*, points very much towards an arm's-length relationship between the universities and business in terms of management development. The first of the few courses was jointly established in 1966 between the universities of Münster and Mannheim. It is now run by Münster and Konstanz. The seminar lasts for three weeks, is run once per year, and targeted at top managers. The University of Gießen runs an annual two-week seminar with two target groups – senior managers in medium-sized companies and middle managers in large companies. The Technical University of Aachen organizes seminars for technical managers and technology specialists.

The most comprehensive management development programme mounted by a West German university is the *Kontaktstudium Management der Universität Augsburg*. It has been running since 1976 and has much in common with so-called executive, or part-time, management development programmes in the UK. The *Kontaktstudium* is designed for practising managers, and ranks as an official programme of the university, with prescribed studies but optional examinations. It contains a foundation course covering the functional areas of management such as accountancy, marketing, operations management, etc., as well as elements devoted to communications skills, conflict management and problem-solving. Sessions are held in the evenings, at weekends, and in one-week blocks, on the premises of the university. The programme is designed on the modular principle, with modules lasting from 10 to 50 hours, building up to 'sequences'. 500 hours in an appropriate set of 'sequences' complete the programme. Interested participants can then opt to take an examination, and successful candidates receive the *Kontakstudienbrief Management der Universität Augsburg*.

Medium-sized companies without the appropriate human, physical and financial resources at their disposal are obliged to look outside the firm for their management development opportunities.

There are in West Germany scores of private organizations offering a plethora of courses in what could loosely be termed management development. Programmes vary in length, content and quality. They are run mostly in hotels. Many of the courses mounted by private organizations are frequented by managers from medium-sized companies and a few by managers from small firms. Fees are, of course, payable.

The cost of courses begins to become significant for medium-sized and small companies, and reduced fees are an undoubted attraction provided that the programmes on offer are equally good. This is very much the case with the management development programmes offered by the West German Chambers of Industry and Commerce. Since all companies involved in 'trade' (*Gewerbe*) must be members of their local chamber and must therefore pay membership fees, the value-for-money courses held under the aegis of the chambers are very popular.

The chambers offer a range of development courses aimed at all levels of management, from entrepreneurs to lower management. Many of them also possess their own short-course centres, some of which are located in attractive countryside and are lavishly equipped.

As is well known, the chambers are intimately involved in initial vocational training (*Ausbildung*), *inter alia* through their inspection of companies training apprentices and the setting of examinations for the apprentices. Moreover, they actually run courses as well as set examinations for further vocational training or 'upgrading' (*Fortbildung*). Therefore, the recent extension of their work into management development (*Weiterbildung*) would appear to be a natural progression. It must, however, be pointed out that management development is not an obligation which is specifically imposed upon them by the Chambers' Act of December 18th, 1956.

The chambers claim to have very sensitive radar, especially for the development needs of medium-sized and small companies, by dint of their close contacts with firms of all sizes and types. Indeed, some of them see their most valuable contribution to lie in the detection of current management development trends in the large companies and the subsequent provision of similar programmes for medium-sized and small companies. All of the development courses organized by the chambers are open to all member companies.

The Munich Chamber of Industry and Commerce, for example, runs its management development programmes in the foothills of the Alps, at

Westerham (affectionately known as West Ham after the English football club). Examples of courses targeted directly at medium-sized companies are those on sales planning, recent developments in production and distribution, and changing from authoritarian to participative management styles[35]. Sometimes, the Munich Chamber combines with other chambers in southern Germany to lay on courses which appeal to companies outside its own catchment area.

Also catering for the needs of medium-sized and small companies, where the latter can be attracted at all, are the *Bildungswerke* in the individual federal states, some of which have so-called 'Management Academies' attached to them. These educational establishments are funded mainly by employers' associations, individual companies, and to a lesser extent by the states themselves, and the fees charged for their courses[36]. They exist primarily because the employers' associations did not want to be totally reliant on the chambers for the provision of vocational opportunities at all levels. Since the employers' associations fund the *Bildungswerke* voluntarily, and not by reason of a federal Act, they can exercise much more direct influence over their activities.

Again, some 80 per cent of the management development courses organized by the *Bildungswerke* are single-company programmes. They are run on the premises of a particular company or in hotels. The courses are staffed by professors from universities or polytechnics, and especially by senior managers and trainers from large companies, in accordance with the cascade principle. Here, experienced staff from the large companies permit their know-how to flow down to managers in medium-sized companies in particular. Many of the courses tend to focus on behavioural or presentation skills, with a few devoted to selling techniques. Indeed, the courses on selling skills are virtually the only ones that succeed in attracting participants from small companies because the lessons learned are perceived as being immediately applicable.

In interviews recently conducted in West Germany, an attempt was made to establish why small companies should display so little interest in management development. The reasons appear to be connected with the entrepreneur mentality. The owners of the small firms do not go on courses themselves because they are too involved in the running of their companies, and they harbour serious doubts as to whether anyone can teach them anything about their particular line of business. Therefore, they do not encourage their staff to attend courses either. Unless the need is patently obvious, as with negotiating or selling skills, the employees in their turn develop a kind of tunnel vision in relation to their particular task: provided the boss is satisfied with their performance, then they are as well.

The usual excuses for neglect of management development which are put forward by small companies in all countries, i.e. lack of time and lack of money, possibly possess even less validity in West Germany than elsewhere. As for lack of time, West German managers have six weeks' holiday per year in addition to the large number of public holidays celebrated in many parts of the country; as for lack of money, many of the small companies are extremely profitable.

The whole issue of management development in West Germany must be viewed within the broader context of continuing education for the entire citizenry. 'Lifelong learning' (*lebenslanges Lernen*) has become a popular slogan, and it is claimed that every year 25 per cent of the population between the ages of 19 and 65 take part in some form of continuing education, including management development[37]. Unfortunately, however, some of the trends are not encouraging. There appears, for example, to be a growing reluctance among unskilled workers, i.e. those without any vocational training at all, to join in continuing education. The participation rate among this group fell from 14 per cent in 1979 to only 8 per cent in 1985. Similarly, the participation rate in continuing education for those with only *Hauptschulabschluß* (the equivalent of 5 CSE passes) is six times lower than for those educated to the *Abitur* standard. In addition, there are significantly higher participation rates for men rather than for women, for the employed rather than the unemployed, and for young people rather than the older age groups[38].

One idea which has been put forward to achieve more equality of opportunity for continuing education is that of *Bildungsurlaub*, i.e., '(Extra) paid holidays for self-improvement'. The broad concept itself has found favour with many bodies in West Germany but there has been a signal failure to define what the term really means. *Bildungsurlaub* has formed part of the DGB (West German equivalent of the British TUC) Basic Programme since 1963. The issue has been discussed in a number of working papers by all the main political parties at federal level. Five of the individual federal states as well as West Berlin have passed different forms of legislation on the subject[39], and in one form or another it has become part of a limited number of tariff agreements between a few of the 17 trade unions and their negotiating counterparts, the employers' associations. As yet, however, there are no federal guidelines covering the whole country[40]. Questions of how much extra paid holiday per annum, and what constitutes 'self-improvement' are still awaiting satisfactory answers by the majority of companies. Hence reactions to the concept of *Bildungsurlaub* by those firms not yet affected by either legislation or tariff accord are totally predictable. 'Look, we can take care of initial vocational training for our apprentices. We also see to it that those of our employees who seem capable of taking on more responsibility are given further vocational training or upgrading. In addition, we provide management development at all levels where we think that it's mutually beneficial – to the company and to the individual manager. But we don't see why we should give any employee of ours extra paid holidays to go to Macedonia for a month to study Greek icons!'

PRESENT PROBLEMS

There are currently in West Germany three main problem areas associated with the education, training and development of managers, concern about which is by no means limited to the present day but extends to the future as well. These are the issues of women in management, manager mobility, and graduate unemployment.

West Germany has at its disposal a large, highly educated female workforce, 38 per cent of all employed persons being women[41]. But females are very much conspicuous by their absence in top and senior management, and strongly under-represented in middle and lower management.

In 1983, 46.4 per cent of school-leavers with the *Abitur* or *Fachhochschulreife* qualification were female, and there were in the same year some 482 000 women at universities and polytechnics, i.e. 37.7 per cent of the total student population. Examining the statistics relating to subjects perhaps most immediately associated with management, in 1983, 79 000 women were reading the economic and social sciences at university and 12 016 engineering. In 1982, 200 of the 1300 doctorates in the economic and social sciences were obtained by women, and 20 of the 1000 doctorates in engineering[42].

Exactly what happens to these large cohorts of highly intelligent females after their education at university and polytechnic is something of a mystery. Of course, some of them marry, but not many begin to produce babies. As has already been noted, West Germany currently holds the world record for the lowest number of children per woman. Nor do women enter management in anything like representative numbers. Interviews on this issue conducted by the author in a sample of West German companies pointed to very low numbers of females in management positions at all levels, the most-quoted reason being that a woman had to be twice as good at her job as a man before she became a manager. The same criterion holds good for promotion further up the management ladder. But the most reliable statistics on women in management are to be located in a survey published in 1986 by FIDA, the society for the promotion of scientific research into the position of women in international co-operation[43]. From May to August 1982, FIDA sent out 4000 questionnaires to a representative selection of companies – large, medium and small, in manufacturing industry and in the services sector. Fewer than 10 per cent of the questionnaires, i.e. 398 in total, were returned and completed. Crushing indifference to the issue of women in management in West Germany is, therefore, the first inference that could be drawn from the evidence of the response rate alone.

Most of the responses came from the chemical industry and the food industry (13 per cent each). Next followed the services sector in general with 12 per cent, including financial services with 11 per cent. However, the average number of women employed in the companies responding was slightly lower, at 33 per cent[44], than the average for female employment throughout West German companies as a whole (38 per cent).

The findings of the survey reveal that the percentage of women in management positions at the individual levels of the hierarchy takes the form of a pyramid (see Fig. 5.4). The higher the position in the management structure, the smaller the percentage of females[45].

The main reasons given in the FIDA survey for the low number of women in management positions are firstly that the traditional role perception of the woman in West German society – that of the 3 Ks (*Kinder, Kirche, Küche,* i.e. 'children', 'church,' 'kitchen') is changing only slowly, and this is reflected in companies (48 per cent of responses). Secondly, the nature and scope of a woman's professional life take second place to her family duties (31 per cent). Thirdly, there are too few female applicants for management positions (28 per cent). Fourthly, too few women are vocationally qualified (17 per cent). Finally, women interrupt their working life for too long in order to rear children (16 per cent)[46].

Fig. 5.4. Percentages of women in management positions in the various levels of the West German industrial hierarchy.

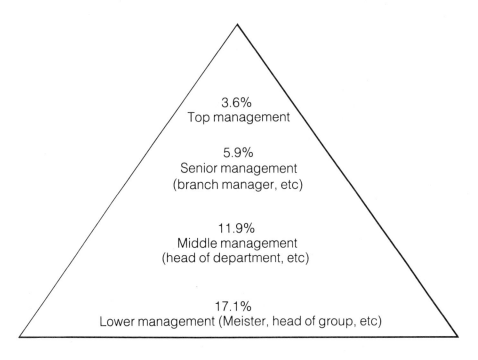

3.6%
Top management

5.9%
Senior management
(branch manager, etc)

11.9%
Middle management
(head of department, etc)

17.1%
Lower management (Meister, head of group, etc)

Source: Frauen als Führungskräfte in der Wirtschaft, FIDA

What should be done about the situation was examined by the same survey. The most-favoured solution was an improvement in the vocational counselling of female school-leavers and their parents (38 per cent of responses); the creation of better conditions for working parents (31 per cent); abolition of anti-female prejudice by information and enlightenment within the company (23 per cent); experimentation with new career patterns, i.e. a second course of training after the child-rearing phase, (20 per cent); private industry ought to implement its own promotion programmes targeted at women (18 per cent)[47].

What should *not* be done is perhaps the most revealing finding of all after the disappointing response rate. The highest degree of rejection was met by the following suggestions: an Office of Equality should be established, with powers of intervention similar to those of the Federal Cartel Office (36 per cent of responses); an Anti-Discrimination Act should be passed (35 per cent); there should be minimum employment quotas for women in companies (34 per cent); equality commissions should be set up in companies (22 per cent); special employment programmes for women should be implemented by the Federal Government (17 per cent)[48].

The FIDA survey separates out some of the replies by male respondents from those by females, and male chauvinism is not difficult to detect in several of the former. Two will suffice as illustration: 'Mothers just don't belong in a factory or an office but with their children, because children have to be brought up, and our society needs new generations with good, bourgeois values'. 'Do women really want to be equal with men? Leave the weaker sex as it is. As they are now, women are just fine for us men'[49]. Both these responses came from owners of companies, and as long as such attitudes are prevalent among the decision-makers, women in West Germany will have to wait some considerable time before they achieve equality of representation at any of the levels of management, let alone the uppermost ranks.

The second problem area identified as affecting management in West Germany today is that of lack of mobility. The problem is by no means confined to managers but is endemic in the entire work-force.

Perhaps the main reason for the lack of mobility lies in the fact that West Germans are essentially creatures of their region, and not of the nation. Germany was a latecomer as a nation, with unification not being achieved until 1871. Many would in fact argue that the nation was not so much unified as taken over by Bismarck's Prussia. The result is that even today a Bavarian does not feel at ease living and working outside Bavaria: the same applies in equal measure to, say, a citizen of the state of Hamburg. Emotional loyalties lie first with the region.

The mobility problem was perhaps further exacerbated several years ago by a famous case which came before the courts. A man achieved promotion within his company and informed his wife that his new post involved a transfer from Hamburg to Munich. The wife protested that she did not want to leave Hamburg, but the husband countered that, as head of the family, he was responsible for their upkeep, and this entailed his choice of their domicile. The case went all the way to the Federal Constitutional Court in Karlsruhe, where a decision was reached in favour of the wife. The husband could not force her to transfer to Munich since one of her basic rights was affected, i.e. that of her freedom of movement (Article 11, Section (1), *Grundgesetz*, 'Basic Law').

A further determinant in the lack of mobility of West Germany's work-force can be found in company paternalism. In the late 1940s and the 1950s, when a chronic housing shortage coincided with a labour shortage, West German firms began to offer subsidized rents in company flats as a means of attracting workers. Whole areas of certain towns were bought up by companies, and flats were built for white and blue-collar workers alike. Now the housing shortage and the labour shortage have long since passed, but low-rent company apartments still act as a disincentive for employees to change company. Holiday entitlement also rises with length of company service, as do other perquisites such as the benefits from occupational pension schemes, very few of which are transferable.

Factors not attributable to the company are also involved. There has been an oversupply of housing in Germany since the mid-1970s, with the result that house prices have actually fallen in some areas over the past ten years. Moreover, doubts about whether the spouse could procure as well-paid a job in the new town, physical separation from parents and grandparents, even concern about waiting-lists at a new tennis club are factors not to be overlooked.

All this contributes to a conviction, which is widespread throughout the country, that if employees change company three or four times in a working life they are *nicht seriös* ('unprofessional'). In the land of the professional, the expert, the *Techniker*, there can be no more damning indictment!

Accordingly, of the 12 000 positions available in top management in West Germany, 1500 of which become free every year, only 200 to 230 are ever advertised[50]. The rest are filled by companies internally. At the level below, i.e. that of senior management, there are estimated to be some 170 000 posts in the country. Here the annual turnover amounts to approximately 34 000 posts, 25 000 of which are filled internally. Therefore, some 75 per cent of top and senior management posts are taken up by promotion from within. The figure is even higher for large companies, many of whom have any number of suitable candidates to choose from. The vast majority of the small number of top and senior posts are thus available in medium-sized and small companies.

Top management mobility in West Germany is not exactly enhanced by the generous salaries, including loyalty bonuses, paid to the incumbents of such posts, particularly in the large companies. Average remuneration in the mid-1980s was in excess of DM 1 million for each of the members of the management boards at Altana, Bertelsmann, Krones, Springer, Volkswagen, Deutsche Bank, Gruner + Jahr, Lemförderer Metallwaren, Daimler-Benz, BHF-Bank, Rheinmetall, and Bayer[51].

Indeed, managers at all levels in West Germany, even in medium-sized companies, have few reasons to complain about their salaries. The typical remuneration structure for a manufacturing company, with a turnover of DM 150 million and 1000 employees, in the mid-1980s was: top manager DM 320 000; senior manager DM 240 000; middle manager DM 140 000; lower manager DM 90 000[52]. It will be noted that the company hierarchy is faithfully reflected in the salaries of the managers at the various levels. Salary levels also affect the mobility of the blue-collar work-force, but in a different way. Here there is a two-stage system of salary negotiations. At the first stage, minimum rates of pay are set in negotiations between one of the 17 trade unions and the corresponding employers' association, either for the whole country or the whole region. The translation of these minima into actual earnings then takes place at plant level in bargaining between local management and the local works council. The outcome is, almost inevitably, that actual earnings for the same job do not vary significantly from company to company. Thus the main incentive is lacking for an individual to move from one company to another even within the same region, let alone outside 'his' or 'her' region.

There is little hope that the mobility problem will be solved in West Germany in the foreseeable future. Even the record numbers of unemployed, including managers, in the late 1970s and early 1980s failed to make a significant impact.

The third problem area in West Germany today also concerns the labour market, but it does not affect so much existing managers as aspiring ones. As indicated earlier, it is the very grave problem of graduate unemployment.

The *Techniker* tradition of education at polytechnics and universities, coupled with lengthy periods of study, has as its natural corollary a one-start system in society. As was seen earlier in the case of the humanities graduates in the Hamburg area, if a young person is educated in a particular discipline, he or she is expected to earn a living on the basis of those studies. Once a lawyer, always a lawyer; once a shoe salesman, always a shoe salesman. The opportunities for a change of direction after completion of studies, or even vocational training, are limited in the extreme.

If, in addition, there is in the country a legal right of entry to any university to study any subject where there is no *numerus clausus* in operation provided a young person is in possession of the *Abitur* qualification; and if, as a result of larger age cohorts and higher participation rates, university expansion proceeds at the rate which was demonstrated earlier, resulting in today's so-called 'mass universities', then the necessary prerequisites for graduate unemployment are given. All that is needed to make it a reality is a recession, or changes in economic patterns. Over the past decade, West Germany has witnessed both.

The outcome has been a steep and continuing rise in graduate unemployment. Whereas in 1980 there were on average 2 university graduates competing for every job, in 1985 the figure was 8[53]. Registered as unemployed at the end of 1984 were some 29 000 graduates who trained as teachers, 22 000 as engineers, 13 000 as economic or social scientists, 6500 as natural scientists, 3700 as doctors of medicine or dentists, and 2300 as lawyers[54].

Looking more closely at those graduates who would most probably have sought to enter management, from 1973 to 1985 the figure for unemployed economic scientists from universities grew by 619 per cent. The corresponding figure for unemployed economic scientists from polytechnics increased from 1975 to 1985 by 316 per cent[55].

Currently, very little is being done in West Germany to alleviate the problem. The idea has been mooted that a *numerus clausus* should be imposed for the economic sciences in an effort to curtail the supply, which is at present putting some 13 000 fresh economic scientists on to the labour market every year[56]. Some retraining courses for graduates from all disciplines are being run by the Federal Institute of Labour (*Bundesanstalt für Arbeit*). In addition, the federal government in Bonn has made sporadic attempts to persuade individual companies to take on unemployed graduates with a view to retraining, but without success. Graduates are in fact being told they are relatively fortunate that so few of them are unemployed. Whereas 17 per cent of unskilled and 5.9 per cent of skilled workers were without a job at the end of 1985, the figures for polytechnic graduates were 'only' 5 per cent and for university graduates 4.5 per cent[57]. This is, of course, scant consolation, especially when future prospects are considered.

According to the Institute of Labour Market and Vocational Research (*Institut für Arbeitsmarkt und Berufsforschung*), there were in the country in 1980 a total of 1 501 000 university graduates, 874 000 of whom will still be employed in the year 2 000. There will be an additional demand for 627 000 graduates by the end of the century because of retirements in the interim. But in the year 2000 the new supply of graduates will be 2 109 000. If the 627 000 graduates for whom there is a forecast of demand are subtracted from this new supply, then by the year 2 000 West Germany will have 1 482 000 university graduates for whom extra jobs will have to be found, total university graduate supply having reached 2 983 000![58].

Patterns of university graduate employment are also forecast to change. Hitherto, the vast majority of these graduates have found employment in the public services, and not in the private sector. But in view of the large degree of indebtedness of the public services at all three levels of government – federal, state and commune – and the increasing number of university graduates, it is highly improbable that previous take-up rates of such graduates by the public services, of some 60–70 per cent, will ever be achieved again[59].

The private sector is, therefore, expected to absorb the vast majority of these graduates, and the marked trend towards the academization of management has indeed been noted. But the West German economy would have to achieve phenomenal growth rates from now until the end of the century to create sufficient jobs for all graduates. Small wonder, then, that successful *Abitur* candidates are increasingly reluctant to study at university at all, or if they do so, not until they have taken out an insurance policy in the form of a traditional apprenticeship.

FUTURE CONCERNS

A total of almost one and a half million unemployed graduates by the end of the century is in itself a horrifying prospect for any advanced society to have to contemplate. What is more, it is open to question whether West Germany has not only got the numbers wrong in management education, but the direction as well. Is West Germany currently growing the type of manager who will be capable of meeting the challenges of industry and commerce in the twenty-first century?

In 1983, Bruce Nussbaum, co-editor of *Business News*, published his celebrated book, *The World after Oil*[60]. In the chapter devoted to Europe in general and West Germany in particular, he writes: 'The technological base that underpinned Germany's Economic Miracle is quietly becoming obsolete. Like a speeding car that shoots off a pier and hesitates that one moment before plummeting into the sea, West Germany is today a nation confidently moving through the twentieth century unaware of the economic catastrophe that has already befallen it .... For West Germany is fast losing the high-tech race to Japan, the United States and perhaps even France. It may soon find itself a second-rate economic power, the new "sick man of Europe".[61]'

Nussbaum argues that the twenty-first century has already begun in the sense that two locomotives, micro-electronics and bio-technology, are quickly pulling the world into a new era. Whoever falls behind in the race for these two key technologies will be unable to keep abreast of other nations. 'Germany today is a nation that cannot make the change from mechanical engineering to bio-engineering. It cannot make the leap from precision-engineering, the machines of yesterday, with their thousands of moving parts and motors, to the throwaway electronic devices of today and tomorrow. It cannot make the change from petroleum-based chemicals to biologically produced pharmaceuticals.[62]'

Shortly after the publication of Nussbaum's book, Dr Konrad Seitz, head of planning in the West German Foreign Office, wrote an article in *Der Spiegel* responding to the criticism[63]. He admitted that the general line of Nussbaum's thinking was correct, even if the pace of change was not so rapid as the American believed. Seitz called for a concerted effort between West German industry, state bodies, science and the media to close the technology gap, and made four specific demands: more computers in schools; a policy unit to co-ordinate university research;

state loans to sponsor research and development; and an efficient system in the country for raising venture capital.

The stir which Nussbaum's criticism caused in West Germany at the time can be gauged from the fact that, nine numbers later, *Der Spiegel* addressed the same problem again[64], this time in a leading article. The leader opened with a list of West German traditional industries in trouble, quoted Nussbaum extensively, and reminded readers that West Germany had been awarded only 12 Nobel Prizes for science since the Second World War, with a number of these referring back to discoveries in the 1930s, as compared to one single university in the United States, Stanford, with 9 Nobel Prizes. The article concluded by quoting the managing director of Hewlett-Packard West Germany, who stated that the country needed its own equivalent of the American Apollo programme in order to revitalize industry.

Nussbaum obviously struck a raw nerve in West Germany, and large companies there took the criticism seriously. They, too, realized that, despite the large amounts of money they were spending on research and development at home, they were failing to close the technology gap. Two clear strategies have emerged in the meantime which are aimed at returning to the forefront of technology: international co-operation in research and development; and purchases of overseas companies by cash-rich West German firms.

In the field of micro-electronics, Siemens began in 1984 to co-operate with Philips on a programme to develop the one-megabit chip[65]. Subsequently, Siemens came to an agreement with Toshiba to realize an even larger version, the four-megabit chip. By the end of the 1980s, Siemens plans to have spent some DM 100 million on the research and development in addition to DM 1.4 billion on plant for the actual production of the chips.

Purchases overseas by West German companies, especially in the United States, had begun even before Nussbaum's book was published. In 1981, Hoechst paid $ 50 million to the Harvard and Massachusetts General Hospital to enter the field of gene splicing. In return for the cold cash, Hoechst not only obtained first claim on all patents coming out of the research but also the right to train its own scientists in bio-engineering at Harvard. According to Nussbaum, the Hoechst decision not to set up its genetic engineering research in any of the West German universities or research institutes '... was seen as a blot on the honor of the nation'[66]. When Hoechst later announced that it was to set up a small genetics laboratory in Japan, West German academia was reported to be 'livid'[67].

In 1986, Hoechst made a much larger purchase in the United States, when it bought up Celanese for $2.85 billion to become the world's largest chemicals group. In doing so, it surpassed its large German rivals, BASF and Bayer[68].

In 1985, BASF had bought Inmont for $ 1 billion. It also took over three smaller companies and reorganized its American operations under a newly formed BASF corporation.

Bayer has traditionally been strong in the United States market, which accounts for some 25 per cent of total sales. In 1986, it bought back the right to use its own name and trademark there, which it had forfeited after the 1914–18 war. This exercise in orderly housekeeping cost $ 25 million.

Siemens in 1986 paid $ 420 million for parts of GTE, an American telecommunications company, and in 1985 it acquired or raised its stake in a handful of smaller American firms. Its capital investment in North America totalled DM 727 million in 1985, compared with DM 469 million in Western Europe, excluding West Germany[69].

According to figures by the American Commerce Department, West Germany's direct investment in America had in 1986 a book value of more than $ 14 billion. In excess of 2000 German-owned firms are active there, employing some 400 000 people[70]. The push to catch up in the fields of micro-electronics and bio-technology, the restrictions on the growth of the larger companies at home by the West German Federal Cartel Office, and the strength of the DM against the dollar have all contributed to making internationalization, especially in the United States, an extremely attractive proposition for West German companies.

Purchasing a company abroad is one thing: running it successfully is something quite different. Although it is often possible to employ a certain number of the indigenous population as managers, strategic decisions will inevitably be taken by German managers back home. Of the chairmen of the management boards of the 20 top West German companies in 1987, only 11 had either studied or worked abroad. Twenty per cent of the top managers at the Dresdner Bank had overseas experience, and 33 per cent at Siemens[71].

Nor is the picture likely to change radically in the future. In fact, it could get much worse. In 1985, only 1.8 per cent of all West German students were attending a university abroad, and the vast majority of these were foreign language students[72]. To take just one example, of the 3000 West German students in France in 1985, over 2000 were studying the French language, and only 150 were reading one of the economic sciences.[73].

We know, however, that very few if any of these foreign language students will find employment in West German companies, as was evidenced by the survey of the humanities graduates in Hamburg, to which reference was made earlier. Equally, we know that there are no MBA students 'made in West Germany', who might have been expected to possess at least a nodding acquaintance with the subject of international management. We know also that very few West Germans go abroad to take the MBA qualification, thus missing out on many networking opportunities with their peer groups overseas. Although certain courses such as the European Business Studies Programme at the polytechnics of Reutlingen and Schloß Reichartshausen and, more recently, the Business Economics Programme at the new and private University of Koblenz insist on study periods abroad, these are exceptions which merely serve to expose West Germany's future deficiency in international management expertise. We can conclude, therefore, that comparatively little is being done at the level of higher education to produce the international managers that West Germany will need in the future to run its business interests abroad.

If, then, a pronounced degree of parochialism is to be detected in management education in the polytechnics and universities, what is being done about international management in West German companies? We have seen that management development for lower managers is function or area-specific. Moreover, we have seen that development for the middle tier of management is company-specific. We have also seen that, although management development for senior managers embraces courses on the company environment, considerations are restricted mostly to the environment within West Germany.

The initiative for education or development in international management is therefore left to the individual. Here he or she can be assisted by the Carl Duisberg Society in Cologne, which arranges a study/work programme in the United States for some 100 West Germans per year; or by the American Chamber of Commerce in Germany, which runs a similar programme for some 80 persons every year[74]. The cost of both these programmes is, however, borne mainly by the participants themselves. The most that West German companies are apparently prepared to do is to guarantee that participants will not lose their jobs during the interim abroad[75].

West Germany's continuing neglect of an international dimension to the education and development of her managers appears to be all the more incomprehensible if, in addition to her substantial and growing business interests abroad, the fact is taken into consideration that some 36 per cent of GNP is accounted for by exports. This neglect can only be explained by the country's strict adherence to the *Techniker* tradition of functional management and the concomitant rejection of education, training and development in general management, together with its allied discipline of international management.

CONCLUSION

There can be no denying that the West German tradition has served the country well over the decades since the end of the Second World War. On any measure of economic success, West Germany has performed well, and many of her citizens are enjoying the benefits of that success in an affluent society. But this high level of performance has been achieved in conditions of steady state or continuous change.

The burning question today is: could the West Germans become victims of their own success? Their reluctance to change a winning formula in the education, training and development of their managers is perfectly understandable in view of their past record. But this same approach may be less well suited to radical shifts in markets or types of technology, i.e., conditions of discontinuous change, which, as we have seen, are already beginning to affect the country's economy.

If cash-rich West German companies outside the high-technology sector also decide that internationalization of their business interests provides the best hedge against the vagaries of discontinuous change – and there are already signs that this is happening, with Bertelsmann taking over RCA Records and Doubleday, the American publisher, to become the world's largest media group[76] – then the education, training and development of international managers will become an urgent necessity. How West Germany can break the dominance of the *Techniker* tradition and begin to produce sufficient numbers of generalist managers with an international background is the problem which should be occupying the minds of the planners in the various ministries of education and the thinkers in the development departments of West German companies. To date, there is scant evidence to suggest that this is in fact the case.

6 GREAT BRITAIN

BY CHARLES HANDY

For a long time common sense, character and background were, for the British, more important for managers than any kind of formal training or qualification. Experience was the only worthwhile school and personal introduction or reference more valuable than any qualification.

The 'manager', as a job or role, has not until recently been seen as a high status occupation in Britain. Traditionally, in the older British institutions the word 'manager' was used for the more lowly service functions of catering manager or transport manager with the top officials called principals, partners, directors or even permanent secretaries. The British had great colonial administrators but never spoke of them as managers. Business, too, was low status, particularly manufacturing business, and a business manager therefore a low status job in a low status occupation. Business schools were thought to be typing schools in the early days, while commerce was a euphemism for bookkeeping in schools and colleges.

Words convey messages and these words have left their legacy in Britain. It was only after the Second World War that the big corporations in Britain started to think in terms of formal managerial careers, to recruit people as potential managers from the universities and to produce formal training and education. The scene has now changed radically; no longer do British assume that anyone with any sense can manage anything; there is a lot of activity:

- some big corporations expect to spend up to £4 million p.a. on training, excluding the trainer's salaries. Many others spent over £1 million in 1983[1]. This is big money. Only 50 American companies spent more than £1 million in 1986.

- at least 40 companies in Britain have their own management training centres[1].

- eighty per cent of all large companies do some management training, although less than half their managers take part in it[2].

- there are over 70 000 people studying management or business at some level in the polytechnics and colleges of further education[3].

- there are 40 universities offering postgraduate studies of some sort in management or business.

- there is a growing number of educational programmes for managers in government, in schools, in health organizations and in agriculture.

- there are over 12 000 people every year who obtain an undergraduate degree, a postgraduate degree, a Diploma in Management Studies or a Higher National Diploma[3].

Nevertheless, there is a wide consensus that there are many of the 2.75 million people in managerial roles and, of the 90 000 who enter such roles every year who are untouched by any of this activity, that the average UK manager receives one day's training per year (which conceals a wide variety) and that much more needs to be done.

It is also apparent that Britain has a wide variety of approaches but no clear pathway to a managerial career nor a clear philosophy of how management can best be taught, or learnt or developed. Three clear approaches can be distinguished.

- The Corporate Approach

- The Academic Approach

- The Professional Approach

There are values in each, but at present the variety confuses rather than stimulates. A short historical picture is, however, a necessary prelude to a discussion of the three approaches.

THE HISTORICAL BACKGROUND

A few universities had offered a number of commerce degrees in the early 1900s and a few of the bigger companies such as Shell, Unilever and ICI had established training centres in the pre-war years, but any significant interest in the education of managers and potential managers starts after the Second World War.

In 1946 the Administrative Staff College was founded, building on the ideas of the Staff College of Armed Services for officers in mid-career. In 1947 the British Institute of Management was founded and introduced a certificate and a diploma, which in the early 1960s became the Diploma in Management Studies and was taught in technical colleges.

In the 1950s companies like Unilever with its Management Development Scheme started to recruit generalists as well as scientists from universities and the tradition of the annual university recruiting 'milk-round' was started along with the concept of management trainees. More companies started their own internal training centres and began to plan managerial careers for their key people. As Constable and McCormick comment [3] 'relative to the national need, the scale of activity was very small and unfocused'.

In 1960, following the initiative of a small number of leading industrialists, the Foundation for Management Education was established to promote management education and to raise money. In 1963 the Robbins report on higher education recommended that two postgraduate management schools should be built to give added weight to the developments already taking place in universities. Lord Franks was then asked to advise specifically on these two schools. He recommended that they should offer a one-year postgraduate course and a 20-week general management course for practising managers with an eventual output of 200 postgraduates per year from each school. These two schools then went ahead, although not exactly on the lines laid down by Franks, with matching funds from industry and from government.

Over the next 20 years there was considerable growth in the provision of management education and training in the academic secor. Twenty-three universities currently provide undergraduate degrees and 40 offer some form of postgraduate studies. Forty-one polytechnics and colleges provide undergraduate degrees while over 70 offer postgraduate courses including the Diploma in Management Studies. This proliferation of courses, however, still results in relatively small numbers of people. 4500 individuals received undergraduate degrees in 1985; about 2500 obtained postgraduate qualifications from taught and research-based courses and

1800 received diplomas; 8800 in all.

In the colleges and institutions of further education there has also been a proliferation of courses leading to BTEC and NEBSS qualifications, courses which provide a good grounding in the basic concepts of business and management but which are not, as yet, seen as fitting into a general pathway of qualifications.

The last twenty years have also seen the growth of the post-experience short course. Constable and McCormick[3] estimate that there were, in 1985, 131 000 participant weeks of training on offer from universities, professional institutes and management consultants or private institutions, of which 62 per cent were provided by the universities. It is a growth industry with the providers anticipating a 50 per cent growth over the next five years, the major constraint being a shortage of qualified staff.

131 000 participant weeks amounts to about one quarter of a day per year for each practising manager in the UK. Growth, therefore, has clearly not reached saturation point.

In-company management training has also increased exponentially during the last 20 years. Figures are, however, hard to obtain since few organizations keep detailed statistics. Mangham and Silver's 1986 survey[2] showed that there were still large areas where no training was done. Over half of all companies surveyed had no plans for any training in 1986 – a figure which included a fifth of all those employing more than 1000 people. In those companies which did do training only about one-third of their managers participated and in the larger companies less than 10 per cent of senior managers received any training in 1986.

Another feature of the British scene is the large number of professional institutes, ranging from architects to accountants to personnel management, whose work requires some understanding of business or management and who therefore make some knowledge or experience of this a part of their qualifications. Fifty-six of the professional bodies provided information to Constable and McCormick in 1986. In total they had 1.1 million members. For half of the institutes, management studies represented less than 15 per cent of the total study time, but for the other half it represented up to 75 per cent of the total time required of students.

Much of the training is common in nature but there is no agreement, even among the Consultative Council of Professional Management Organizations (CCPMO), on a common core. Nevertheless, over 70 000 students in 1987 were studying for the examinations of these organizations, examinations which all pay at least some attention to business and management concepts.

THE NUMBERS GAP

The last 20 years has seen an exponential if haphazard growth in the provision of education and training, but more needs to be done. Constable and McCormick[3] estimate that out of a reported total of 2.5–3.0m managers in the UK:

350 000 will be senior managers
800 000 will be middle managers
1 600 000 will be junior and first line managers.

If a 30-year managerial life is assumed, then there will be 90 000 new entrants every year, of whom 35 000 may move on to middle management and 17 500 to senior management. Of those 90 000, only 10 000 get any formal education in management up to degree level or its equivalent, with a further 15 000 picking up some from their studies for professional institutions.

It is likely that once in the company only two out of three will receive any further education and training and that for those that do it will be of the order of one or two days in a year.

A 1987 CBI random survey by Gallup of managers revealed that 36 per cent were currently undergoing formal training in their employer's time and that a further 38 per cent had done so in the last five years, but that the training averaged between only 1 and 5 days.

Forty per cent of this sample have a degree of some sort and just over 50 per cent belong to a professional institute. Although 59 per cent report that an appraisal scheme operates in their company only 13 per cent believe that their company plans their career and provides the necessary training. Only one-quarter of the managers surveyed believe that training will *not* be important for their career, but, looking at it the other way round, 69 per cent do not believe that their company gives sufficient priority to training its employees.

In spite, therefore, of the often dramatic advances in the last twenty years it still seems that approximately half of Britain's younger managers have left education before degree level, that half probably receive no significant formal training after starting work and that prolonged and serious study of business and management is reserved for a few. Britain in 1986 produced 2000 MBAs or postgraduate students compared with 70 000 in America, and perhaps 10 000 equivalents to an undergraduate degree compared with 240 000 in America. America is four times as large but these figures are twenty to thirty times higher.

The conclusion is inescapable that in Britain management education and training *is too little, too late for too few*. The British have rationed something which should be universally available and turned a potential common good into a special reserve. What should be a prereqisite of all managers has become a perk for the minority. The result is, in some areas, a spurious élite. The scarcity of MBA graduates, for instance, has created an artificial market with artificial salaries leading many to argue, possibly correctly, that no training can possibly be worth that much more money but then to go on to argue, probably incorrectly, that the training is therefore of no value at all. This has made the MBA course a more contentious issue than it needs to be.

The lack of widespread early education also leads to a pressure for catch-up courses of compressed knowledge. It is not possible to compress the range and depth of a degree course into the two weeks or even two days of many a management programme, resulting in trivialization, banalities and superficiality which, again, lead some to argue, correctly, that these courses achieve little or nothing, and then go on to argue, incorrectly, that no courses or training events are needed.

The large-scale provision of business teaching is below degree level, in NEBS and BTEC courses, for instance, and is located in parts of the education system which the typical graduate or aspiring senior manager never gets near. This again leads to the spurious rationalization that business education is only needed for the bottom layers. The result, today, can often be that the bottom two or three levels in the organization know more about the concepts and ideas of business and management than their superiors who have gone through their education untouched by these things.

More is essential, but it is still unclear what the more should be, at what level, how taught and how recognized. That is where the three strands of the emerging British tradition need to be differentiated.

THE THREE APPROACHES

Britain today provides three different tracks for the aspiring manager in business – the corporate, the academic and the professional. They are not mutually exclusive, for it is possible to try to combine any two of them, but nor are they easily compatible, for none really accepts the relevance of the others. The result is too often confusion.

The corporate approach is akin to the Japanese system. Organizations recruit people on leaving education and then provide them with a mix of training and early experience geared to a long-term career in the organization. The experience is usually confined to one function, the tradition being that the move into general management comes late in one's career. Only then, it is felt, should the training start to concentrate on general principles of management. Until then the training has usually been company-specific and function-specific ('this is the way we do this in this company and in this function!'). Such training carries no credentials and, indeed, is not regarded as being particularly valid outside the company.

In years gone by many of the larger organizations, the clearing banks for instance, recruited people direct from school at the age of 16. Today these organizations recruit from the universities and the polytechnics. Most of them would admit that they over-recruit because they expect that some will leave after a few years, although they would hope to retain the best. This is an explicit recognition of the fact that the thirty or so of Britain's large corporations have for many years been the effective training schools of British managers. The ranks of Shell, Unilever, IBM, ICI and other corporate giants have now been joined in this role of preparatory organizations by the consultancy firms and some of the bigger merchant banks.

In fact, most of the companies now recruiting from universities have developed their own brands of initial training and apprenticeship in recognition of the fact that a demonstrated involvement in training is an aid to recruitment.

The academic approach is a broad imitation of the American tradition. In America the great majority of would-be managers acquire a grounding in business and management concepts at a university business school before joining or soon after. An undergraduate or postgraduate degree in business is becoming almost a prerequisite to a business career in that country. Although some degrees (MBAs from Harvard and Stanford and the other top ten schools) can command premiums, most MBAs are regarded as a form of essential homework rather than as certificates of excellence.

In Britain it is now increasingly possible to study business at college, polytechnic, university or university-based business schools. There is a wide variety of certificates and degrees, ranging from the sub-degree certificates of BTEC and the Higher National Diploma through to one-year and two-year postgraduate MBAs.

It is, however, very unclear what status any of these courses and qualifications has in the eyes of employers, nor is it always obvious how they relate to each other. An MBA for instance is more truthfully a post-experience course taught to graduates with four or more years of work experience rather than an advanced course built on top of an undergraduate degree in business. In fact, most MBA courses would prefer that the student had *not* already studied business at undergraduate level and most undergraduate courses would prefer that the subject had *not* been taken at sub-degree level in school or college.

Charting a path through the apparent jungle of the academic study of business is not, therefore, easy at present for the young men or young women; nevertheless the demand is there, with undergraduate courses in business or accountancy more oversubscribed than any others in university catalogues of degree courses.

The professional approach is one more easily understood by the British, who have always preferred to earn while they learn, a preference made possible in the last thirty years by all the traditional professions who now pay a salary rather than charge a fee to their apprentices.

The professional approach is a mixture of tutored work experience (articles) with formal study leading to a graded series of qualifications, normally ending with membership of an institution.

There are many professional bodies relevant to management and business. The most prestigious of them are probably the institutes of accountants, followed by the members of the Consultative Council of Professional Management Organization (Table 6.1). There are 168 000 people on the registers of the Accountancy Institutes and over 200 000 in the CCPMO bodies. Not all of these are currently active in their professions or currently practising in Britain. In fact very many of them are in managerial roles in business or in other organizations. There is, after all, no conceivable way in which Britain might need 120000 practising auditing accountants (the number of accountants currently thought to be living and working in Britain) when West Germany needs less than 4000 and Japan 6000.

The truth is that accountancy has long been regarded by young people and by employees as an appropriate, high standard and high status preparation for a wide range of jobs in business. Ten per cent of British undergraduates today want to become qualified accountants but only because that is the most obvious, most prestigious and best-remunerated way to prepare oneself with credentials for a general career in business or in management.

Table 6.1: The Consultative Committee of Professional Management Organizations

---

Institute of Chartered Secretaries and Administrators

Chartered Institute of Management Accountants

Institute of Marketing

Institute of Purchasing and Supply

Institute of Personnel Management

Institute of Bankers

Chartered Insurance Institute

Chartered Building Societies Institute

Institute of Industrial Managers

Institute of Administrative Management

There are problems with all three approaches.

The corporate approach is, inevitably, confined to the larger organizations, and is, sensibly, focused on their business and their problems. It is not, therefore, a practical way of educating the generality of managers, most of whom do not start life in large companies.

Even if, as an act of corporate generosity and responsibility, these corporations undertook to take in and to train four times as many people as they needed, it is not obvious that what their trainees would learn would always be relevant to the work outside. The ways of large corporations are not always the ways of smaller ones.

In fact, because most of these large organizations are functionally organized, the great bulk of early training and experience is confined to one function, be that marketing or production or finance. There is not, in Britain, the same understanding of the Japanese principle of the horizontal fast-track in which people of managerial potential are deliberately routed through a variety of functions in their early years. The British are more like the Germans, preferring their recruits to learn one thing well before they broaden out into general management. In firms like IBM it can be fourteen or more years before an individual gets profit responsibility. This functional emphasis makes it less necessary to provide a general business education in the early years but also then requires that education is acquired in a rushed and crammed fashion in mid-career, when most people find it more difficult to go back to school and to learn relatively elementary facts, principles and skills.

In other countries, a general business education is a foundation on which any last specialization is built. Ideally a functional specialist thinks like a businessman as well as a specialist. The corporate approach does not always make this possible in the way it is organized at present in most companies.

The academic approach is currently too confused and confusing to employers and to students to be as useful and as recognized as it might be.

Most of the courses have the same list of topics, subject areas and skills. They differ mainly in the level, age and quality of their students and in the calibre of their teachers. These differences are not always apparent to the outside world, with the result that many courses, particularly at the lower end of the academic pecking order, are better than they seem to be and others are, frankly, not as good as they claim to be.

Many of the courses are criticized in Britain, as they are in America, for being too remote from the world of business and of management about which they claim to teach. They are accused of irrelevancy, of ignoring the practical and personal competences, of creating exaggerated ambitions in the minds of their students and of reductionism, of reducing the complexities of management to over-simple rules and principles.

The muted distrust of the academic approach is probably symptomatic of the British preference for practical experience as the school for life which is, in turn, both one cause of and one result of the unusually small percentage of university-educated people in British society. Currently only 14 per cent of 18-year-olds go on to study for a degree (compared with well over 20 per cent in comparable countries) although falling numbers of teenagers will push this up to 18 per cent in a few years. Even this figure is a substantial increase over the figures before the expansion of the universities in the 1970s. As a result, only 12 per cent of those calling themselves managers in the Labour Force Survey of 1985 have degrees (see Table 6.2) although the CBI 1987 more focused sample of *corporate* managers raised that figure to 40 per cent. Most British managers have not themselves experienced any part of the academic approach since leaving school and do not therefore have a very good understanding of it or sympathy for it.

The professional approach has a long history in Britain. The combination of experience and study makes intuitive sense within the pragmatic tradition. Nevertheless, there is also a distrust of professional bodies who are often regarded as closed shop monopolies, protected by law from competition and therefore slow to change. This privileged position of many of the bodies makes their examinations, courses and membership procedures attractive to the young, but not always to employers.

The education within the professional bodies is, naturally, designed to be relevant to the particular interests and duties of each profession. The fact that this education often includes an introduction to business and management and in some cases a detailed knowledge of some aspects of either business or management does not necessarily mean that the courses are a good preparation for business and management. Accountants, for instance, are trained to be accountants, not businessmen or managers. There are in fact some who argue that the accountants' proper

Table 6.2: The education of British managers, 1985

Qualification	Men %	Women %
First higher degree	12.1	12.8
Member of professional institution	6.2	2.5
HNC/HND	5.6	1.4
Nursing or teaching qualification	1.6	13.4
Apprenticeship (completed)	9.6	3.0
ONC/OND, City and Guilds, 'A' levels	24.2	15.2
'O' levels or equivalent	15.0	18.9
CSE below grade 1	1.5	2.2
Other	3.3	4.6
No qualifications	19.1	24.7
Don't know/no reply	1.7	1.2
Total number of men/women	2 541 000	729 000

Source: :Labour Force Survey, GB, 1985
Note: Men aged 16–64; women aged 56–59

caution, inculcated by their training, can be damaging to a spirit of enterprise and initiative in management.

The professional institutes were never intended to be a pathway to general management nor to provide full education for business. An understanding of business is as much as their courses and their examinations seek to achieve before pressing on with their more particular careers. It is not their fault if many of the young use them for a purpose for which they were not intended, as a preparation for management and a career in business. We should not, however, turn our backs on this traditional British way of learning while one works and earns.

VIEWS OF THE FUTURE

The Constable and McCormick report[3] canvassed the views of employers and of individuals on future needs. A summary of their findings is included as an Appendix to this chapter.

Employers were concerned to improve current practices for training and development. If managers are to succeed in the face of growing international competition, new management development processes will need to be created. In general, employers believed that the current provision of management education and training falls well short of what will be required. There was, however, a lot of criticism of the way things are done at present. More of the same will not be right or enough.

There was, amongst employers, a wide consensus that innate ability and job experience are the most important factors in creating an effective manager. In this they were in agreement with employers in all the other four countries. Nonetheless, there was a growing acceptance that education and training can give a further boost to effectiveness. It was also acknowledged that since few managers gain experience outside one function, education and training can help them to get a broader perspective.

The employers agreed that it would be both inappropriate and impossible to make management a controlled profession similar to accountancy and the law. However, to make a managerial career more similar to those of the professions, and to encourage managers to acquire specific competences appropriate to each stage of their careers, were seen as sensible and helpful.

In any expansion of management education and training it was considered important that:

1   there should be more than one level of qualification, with the levels closely attuned to career development and related to on-the-job experience;

2   any system developed should be flexible, allowing for entry at many points, based on higher education and work experience;

3   training should be modular in form and should be so designed that in-house programmes could be combined with external courses. There was

enthusiasm for credit accumulating, covering both in-house and external programmes;

4   the total development process should recognize the value of on-the-job experience which should be an integral part of the development process;

5   there should be minimal emphasis on the acquisition of formal qualifications for their own sake: most employers were interested in the acquisition of specific job-related skills.

Employers also commented to Constable and McCormick's investigators on the structure and characteristics of management education institutions. They supported the view that management schools should remain within academic institutions rather than be entirely independent. Most of them felt that too many places now offer management programmes.

Management schools were seen as relatively weak in terms of their knowledge of industrial and commercial practice and in their international perspective. They were not seen as offering particularly good value for money.

Individuals regarded their managerial career as their own property rather than that of their employers. In particular, decisions to take courses leading to qualifications were overwhelmingly taken personally. It was felt that qualification courses could lead to improved on-the-job performance and to promotion. This interest in qualifications was universal apart from those employed by very large corporations with outstanding reputations for training in particular functional activities.

Individuals anticipate greater managerial mobility between companies in the future. This increases the demand for portable credentials which recognize not only formal management education and training but also accumulated managerial experience. The survey by Constable and McCormick's group showed that not all individuals recognize their own need for education and training and that in many organizations the management culture discourages requests for formal training. The provision by employers of study time was seen as the most valuable contribution which could be made.

Those who had participated in programmes in educational institutions expressed a high level of satisfaction with the outcome as reflected in their career profession.

It is noticeable that the one significant disagreement between companies and individuals concerns the matter of qualifications and portable credentials – individuals want them, companies do not. The difference is understandable. It throws up again, however, the difference between approaches. In spite of what companies *say*, they still hanker after the corporate approach, are alarmed by the consequences for mobility of the professional approach and distrust the purely academic approach. Individuals prefer the professional with the help of the company and of academia where appropriate. All, however, appreciate that experience is enriched by education and improved by appropriate training. Implicitly, if not explicitly, all are recognizing that the world is becoming more intricate, complex and clever and that increasingly clever and knowledgeable people are required to run its organizations. Education is not an occasional perk in these situations; it is an essential foundation, to be focused by training and interpreted in experience.

Constable and McCormick interpreted their findings as a message for more and better management education and training. In particular, they said, future action must address four issues:

1 ensuring an appropriate number of educated and trained new entrants to the managerial population.

2 providing basic knowledge and skills and updating for existing managers who have not benefited from adequate initial business or management education;

3 providing advanced education and training for managers likely to undertake senior management positions;

4 providing continuing training and development throughout the working life of those managers who do receive appropriate initial education and training.

THE WAY FORWARD

Britain's managers need to be better educated and better developed if they are going to run organizations as effectively as those in the other countries of this study. That was the clear conclusion of the study group.

It does not follow from this conclusion that Britain has no competent managers, no effective organizations and no good practice in education or development for managers. Indeed it was the feeling in the other countries that good British managers and good British organizations were often the best there were. The trouble is, it seems, that there are not enough of them, the good are the exceptions that prove a more depressing general rule – that Britain does not bother much about the education and development of her managers, relying instead on a Darwinian belief in the emergence of the strongest and the best. Darwinism, however, is a long, cruel and wasteful process. It is cruel to those discarded and wasteful in that it needs a lot of mistakes to generate a few successes. It will not do for a country in a rapidly changing world.

The diagnosis may be clear, but the treatment is not. There is much that is good in what currently goes on. The good should be built upon, not discarded. There is great variety of provision at present. Variety is desirable in an uncertain world but it needs some pattern to it if it is not to confuse. It is hard, at present, for a young man or a young woman to know how best to prepare for a career in business or management, it is hard for a firm to know what it should expect its new recruits to have done already or to know what resources, programmes or services are available to it to do more. Because it is unclear, too many individuals and too many firms to do nothing.

Any proposal for the future should take advantage of the lessons that can be learnt from the experience of other countries. There are some advantages, after all, in being the pursuer, as the Japanese have long known. There is, however, no one universal treatment available. Each country has its own ways of preparing its managers, ways which reflect the traditions and the culture of that society. Imported methods seldom spread but remain, if they survive at all, as rather rare and even exotic plants. American-style business schools, for instance, have been started in Britain, France and Japan. In all these countries the individual schools are successful and over-subscribed, but they have not spread to the rest of the culture. Britain must, therefore, in learning from the others, be conscious of her own culture and traditions, and particularly of the professional tradition which seeks to marry study and practice, which allows young people to earn while they learn and which looks for proof of competence as well as knowledge.

In all the professions:

- a knowledge of the basics of the profession is required of the applicant before or soon after entry;

- a period of practice under supervision, supplemented by study, is required of all;

- the practitioners are also teachers and the teachers or academics are also practitioners:

- there is a code of effective practice and a code of ethical behaviour;

- there is a central source of information and recognized ways, including official leave, for practising members to update their knowledge;

- study is respected and continual reading of the professional literature is regarded as essential.

It is, on the face of it, strange that the British never tried to apply the procedures of professionalism to management. Perhaps they feared that management might become a closed shop, but we now know that there is no way in which entrepreneurs could or should be stopped from entrepreneuring or natural managers prevented from emerging at any stage or level in life. It is strange that, as a result, unlike almost any other important job or position, there is no proficiency test for would-be managers, no required training, no apprenticeship. The drivers of our organizations do not even need 'L' plates let alone a licence. Management, it seems, is something that most people are expected to be able to do, like parenting, picking it up as you go along. The other countries do not believe that so important a job can be left to so accidental a process.

The study, therefore, produced a list of the general recommendations – 'an agenda for action' drawing on the experience of the other countries but relating it to the British professional tradition. This agenda is contained in Table 6.3.

This agenda recognized the difference between business education and management development. The provision for each will be different but should be complementary.

BUSINESS EDUCATION

It should be primarily the responsibility of the individual to acquire for

Table 6.3: An agenda for action

(1) Expand the educational base by educating more people more broadly for more years, if possible up to first degree level – following the example of all four countries.

(2) Encourage some form of work experience as part of this education, perhaps during a gap between school and degree studies, perhaps while still at school (via the YTS?) – following the examples of West Germany and France.

(3) Devise a framework for early business education which can give all those likely to have management or business responsibilities a grounding in the core subjects – following the US model, but in a more British way.

(4) Establish a tradition of apprenticeship or 'articles of management' linked with study as the first stage of management development – following Japanese practice, but still within the British tradition.

(5) Encourage leading corporations to set a public standard of five days off-the-job training per year per executive – as in the USA and the big West German companies.

(6) Encourage further good practice in management development by promoting the larger corporations as trendsetters for the rest and as trainers and consultants to suppliers and contractors – as in Japan.

(7) Develop mechanisms for the delivery of training which allows better co-operation between companies and between companies and business schools as in the USA.

(8) Establish an official statistical and information base, statutorily backed if need be, so that government and organizations can know what is happening – as in France.

(9) Find ways to make individual study, reading and learning more corporately respectable – as in Japan and the USA, where education is seen as an investment and its processes and institutions valued.

(10) Encourage firms to look for the best in recruiting, to give individuals early responsibility backed by appropriate help and training and pay them well if they do well – as in the USA.

Source: The Making of Managers, NEDC, London, 1987

himself or herself the necessary understanding of the basic languages and skills of business before he or she starts a management career. As in the traditional professions such a basic understanding is regarded as a prerequisite, it does not qualify anyone to be a manager or businessman, it does not command a premium salary nor entitle one to any role or responsibility. It is a foundation course or a Part I of a bigger qualification.

It is important that there are as many opportunities to do this foundation course as there are people who want to do it. Any rationing at this stage creates a spurious élite once again. There are already all manner of foundation courses, from BTEC up to BA. Some do more than is needed; a few do less. Rationalization is urgently needed to make sense out of the jungle, and some more provision is required. The initial training courses in the large companies could be tailored to meet the requirement and could even be validated by an outside body so that they carry a formal credential. Open learning opportunities could be increased, and more modular courses prepared so that those who want to study while they can, or while they learn other subjects, may be able to do so. The courses and examinations of the professional bodies, including those of accountants, lawyers and architects should desirably build on a similar foundation.

The most straightforward way would be to appoint a validating body (perhaps, in Britain, the Council for the National Academic Awards) which would draw up, after discussion, a common curriculum and agreed standards and would accredit a range of courses as meeting this foundation requirement.

Once such a foundation course was generally available it would be important that it became required by all the relevant professional bodies, by employers and by the providers of more advanced business and management education. If it were also required by the civil service, by health authorities, local government and even by education authorities as a prerequisite to educational responsibility, then Britain would finally begin to have a business literate society, one in which the managers in different sectors could actually talk to each other. Business, after all, is not only as most managers now agree, even primarily about profit but about the delivery of quality goods and services to customers, with profit as the essential means to that end rather than an end in itself. Given that definition, almost everybody in Britain is in business and needs to think like a businessman.

The second stage of education merges with development. Study begins to link with practice and with experience. It should not, however, be a purely random or accidental link but needs to be planned and integrated. One way to achieve this is to encourage a proliferation of second level courses, building on the first level foundation courses, but relating the study to specific areas of work. At one extreme, this means that architects and lawyers would move into their own specialist programmes of courses plus articles or their equivalent; it would mean that the professional management institutions of insurance, banking, personnel or company secretaries would continue to teach and develop their own specialists; it should also mean that the genuine title of MBA should begin to develop its own specialities. If study is to be linked with practice, in the best professional tradition, in one's early years at work, then that study must relate to that practice and not to roles and occupations some years or even decades ahead. One would expect therefore to find MBA programmes concentrating particularly on functions, such as finance or marketing, or purchasing or international business, others with a particular expertise in certain sectors (information technology, retailing, health management, etc.). Such programmes would be increasingly part-time, would give credits for relevant in-company training, would require certain kinds of practical experience to be provided, projects within the company to be offered, company mentors to be officially licensed and opportunities to study to be protected.

If this were to happen, the MBA or its equivalent would be increasingly accepted as both relevant and useful by employers, an atmosphere of mutual respect and trust would develop between academia and companies, young people would acquire a habit of learning together with credentials to line up to as well as enjoy. Business education would have been successfully linked to management development.

MANAGEMENT DEVELOPMENT

Managerial abilities and competences are best developed from experience. This does not, however, happen automatically. The experience has to be reflected upon, understood and subsequently improved upon if there is to be any true learning beyond the crude 'I won't do *that* again'. The experience, moreover, needs to be of more than one type; the reflection needs to be organized and to be assisted in some way, the scope for improvement needs to be stimulated by opportunities to examine how others do it and, finally, there has to be enough scope for the individual to try out possible improvements and enough tolerance to overlook the occasional mistake in pursuit of improvement. It all adds up to a learning culture with a battery of devices. The Japanese do it most systematically with planned job rotation to broaden the experience, tests, essays, mentors and group discussions to bring reflection and understanding out into the open, study visits at home and abroad to stimulate the search for improvement, together with books, courses and a constant search for a better way, and a long-term view of the future of both individuals and the firm which helps to put any mistakes into perspective. Formal courses have a part but only a small part in this rather subtle process of discovery. Certainly a functional career, an appraisal scheme and a three-week management course are a poor substitute for the Japanese way, yet most British organizations currently do little else.

The subtlety of the total process means that it cannot be easily formalized or easily legislated into effect. The French try to do it that way but probably achieve more outward observance then true inward conversion. In Britain, case-law made fashionable is slower but probably more effective in the end. If the best organizations in Britain claim that one of the reasons they are best is because of the trouble they go to in order to increase the potential and maximize the learning of their people then others will follow. Britain needs therefore some highly visible examples of good practice.

The study group recommended that a group of leading companies should develop a *Charter* of good practice, including a few numbers (percentage spent on training, days per manager and training) as a minimum benchmark, and that these companies should constitute themselves as a *Charter Group* charged with setting the standards for management development and for advocating its course in society at large, with government and with the universities when needed.

Such a Charter might include:

- a corporate development plan
- a commitment to five days minimum off-the-job training per year for every executive
- a personal development plan for every executive
- a tuition reimbursement for approved self-education
- a formal system for experienced-based learning
- integrated study programmes in co-operation with a business school
- distance learning modules, with the Open University or Open College
- language instruction as a routine requirement
- opportunities for executives to teach part-time in business schools
- study visits to competitors and other organizations
- programmes for training suppliers and contractors
- opportunities for specialists to take part-time advanced degrees
- corporate learning programmes for groups of top managers (using their own organization as a live case-study)

The elements of such a Charter are borrowed from the other countries, but together they make an impressive array of learning opportunities. The implied message is clear: if you work for us, we will work for you. It is a message that should attract many of the most talented to what is an increasingly important task – managing changing organizations.

THE INFRASTRUCTURE

A commitment to five days' training or education per year for every manager will mean a lot more training in British companies. Few of them are equipped to provide it on their own. There will need to be more alliances with business schools and colleges, as in the USA, more company training centres and more managers prepared and trained to act as occasional teachers.

In Germany and France the Chambers of Commerce, founded by business, are essentially training organizations providing a range of courses for junior and middle managers and, in Germany, running the dual system of vocational training for young people. There is no equivalent in Britain. One is needed. The Local Employer Networks and Local Collaborative Projects recently established by the Manpower Services Commission offer a possible alternative. To grow into the size that is required, however, they will need resources. It is here perhaps that a statutory tax on business, as in France, might be both necessary and sensible.

The study made it very evident that information on the whole training training scene in business is very rudimentary in Britain compared with the other countries. In France the information is collected regularly because it is required by law and is available centrally from government. Much the same applies to Germany and France. In the USA, as so often in a vast non-system, information is collected by private survey but there are many of those, although they are not always strictly comparable one with another. In Britain there is little official data and the surveys are partial and infrequent.

What we do not value, we do not count. The lack of information is a comment on the low priority put on training in Britain. Now that the priority is changing, more information will be needed. Perhaps, too, we shall start to value it more when we count it more often. A central data base is badly needed so that providers and suppliers of education and training can know where the market is, and so that the market can know what is available. Companies could perhaps be required to provide details of their training expenditure in their annual report, something which they might prefer to a regular return to a government department. It would also help if there was one government department with a clear responsibility for the whole of management education and development.

The main stumbling block, however, to any big increase in the education and training of managers is likely to be the shortage of qualified teachers. It would take too long to treble the number of teachers by the traditional route of research apprenticeship at universities, nor is there any consensus that this is always the best way to prepare a teacher. It would be more useful to follow the traditional professional practice and arrange more practitioner experts to become part-time faculty. It would enrich their own understanding and that of their companies, ensure that more teaching was in line with current practice and would generally make the education and training process more credible to the participants. If firms were encouraged to release them part-time, if they were required to go through a short course on educational method, and if they were given the status of associate faculty it is possible that the supply of teachers could be dramatically increased at small cost to the institutes of education.

The major difficulty to this last proposal may well be the resistance of the existing teachers who may see this as an encroachment on their territory if not a take-over. That would be a pity. Full-time academics will always be both necessary and needed. It is their task to conceptualize the tasks of business and management, to challenge current practice and orthodoxies, to develop a habit of learning in their students and to be the ones who can stand back from the activity of business and management and see it as it really is. As in the traditional professions, academics and practitioners are both needed. Both should respect the other.

APPENDIX:

PERSPECTIVES ON MANAGEMENT TRAINING AND EDUCATION: THE RESULTS OF A SURVEY OF EMPLOYERS*

SUMMARY OF FINDINGS

This report is based on an interview survey of 206 large private and public sector institutions (the 'panel') in September–October 1986. A summary of the results which emerge from the survey is given below.

1. Management development policy

The great majority (85 per cent) of organizations in the survey have explicit management development policies. However, these are the largest organizations in Britain, and the overall result is quite different from that found in the recent study by Mangham and Silver. Moreover most of the policies provided to us[71] were far from comprehensive. Responsibility for initiating these policies was fairly evenly split between the personnel department and the CEO, but responsibility for implementation was more firmly located with the CEO. The panel was far from complacent with only a minority responding positively about their policy's effectiveness.

2. Management training and education methods

Management development methods varied with career stage. At the

* Reproduced, with permission, from the report 'The Making of British Managers' by J. Constable and R. McCormick, BIM, London, 1987.

induction stage, in-company training predominated. At the functional management stage, planned job experience/rotation and external short courses became more important, with some increase in external qualifications. At the stage of transition to general management, external short courses and job experience/rotation were again most common, with the use of external qualifications less marked. The main source of initiative for attending specific programmes came from department/ functional levels within the organization. A request for indications of changed methods in the future produced a wide variety of response, with the two main thrusts being more job rotation and more use of external courses and distance learning.

3. Expenditure on training

Some four-fifths of organizations had an explicit management training budget, set on a range of different bases, and the reported expenditure varied considerably between organizations from under 100 to more than £1000 per manager for the direct costs of training per year. The mean expenditure was £482, although direct training costs should not be seen as a full measure of management development costs.

4. Management career patterns and recruitment

Just over half the organizations had a planned career structure for their managers, but experience in more than one function was uncommon. Management vacancies tended to be filled internally at all levels, although this was least true of senior levels. About a third of the organizations used the external labour market extensively in the sense of recruiting 20 per cent or more of their managers from outside the organization, while a little over a third hardly needed to use the external market. Roughly a third of respondents did not believe that it was essential for candidates for a post to have worked in that function before; this group tended to attach more importance to formal management education than did the rest.

5. Components of managerial competence

Most organizations (61 per cent) defined the qualities looked for in managers by examining jobs separately and specifying the personal qualities required; in 32 per cent of organizations there was an identified set of managerial qualities required by the organization. The key aspects contributing to the development of a good manager were rated on a five-point scale, and inherent personality and job experience were perceived as the most important factors, with various aspects of education and training, namely initial vocational education, in-company training, initial non-vocational education, and external management education, following some distance behind in that order.

6. Internal and external modes of development

There was clear evidence that external and internal modes of developing managers were perceived as complementary. The characteristics rated highly on internal training were thought to be more important, but nevertheless there was an important role for the attributes rated highly through external modes of training. Of the external inputs short courses and consultant provision of in-company training were thought to be the most important. However, the overall role of external inputs was seen as limited, although expected to grow in the future. Forty per cent of respondents felt that their managers would not have the same priorities for external inputs as the organizations, commonly believing that the latter would rate the importance of external qualifications more highly.

7. Towards a programme for management development

In terms of the balance between investment for the future and immediate contribution to the job that management education could bring, almost half said at least 60 per cent of management education should be considered an investment for the future, while a third said at least 60 per cent should be an immediate contribution to the job. Three-quarters of organizations said that it was both desirable and feasible that in-company and external modules should be combined in a programme of management development. On the content of a management education programme, respondents were asked to allocate a percentage reflecting the desired proportion of content to each of four components within an overall total of 100 per cent. The composite percentage breakdown reflected a balance comprised of just under 30 per cent for both specific skills and general skills, and just over 20 per cent for two knowledge dimensions, namely knowledge of management theory and knowledge of the management environment.

Three-quarters of the organizations said that the external component of a management education programme should be carried out on a modular basis with attendance for 3–6 weeks at a time. Thirty per cent of the respondents were also attracted by distance learning programmes.

When asked how they would advice a son or daughter going into management, 57 per cent said they would advise taking any degree followed by employment in a company with an effective internal management development programme, although only slightly less said they would advise some form of business degree at some stage.

8. The demand for management education

More than four-fifths of the respondents said that it was important for the improvement of the quality of British management that a much higher proportion of those with the potential to reach higher levels of management should undergo a formal programme of management education.

Asked how important it was that a programme of management education should lead to a qualification, 29 per cent said it was important, while 41 per cent said not important. Forty-one per cent of respondents felt that demand for management education should be determined by setting a training budget on a per capita basis and discussing each individual's training needs with him/her.

9. Structural dimensions of management education

By 55 per cent to 26 per cent, respondents preferred a number of qualifications, relating to different levels of management, to a single qualification.

By 47 per cent to 41 per cent, respondents thought it desirable for management to move towards the concept of a profession.

By 48 per cent to 37 per cent, respondents preferred a limited number of institutions providing management education to this being done at most higher education institutions.

By 52 per cent to 29 per cent, respondents preferred management education to be integral within higher education rather than separate and privatized.

By 45 per cent to 32 per cent, respondents preferred bespoke to standardized management education programmes.

By 45 per cent to 20 per cent, respondents felt that qualifications are not an adequate means of identifying quality in managers.

By 69 per cent to 13 per cent, respondents felt that institutions of higher education should have a broader role than training for industry.

By 61 per cent to 12 per cent, respondents said they were dissatisfied with the quality of faculty in institutions of higher education.

Respondents rated current aspects of management and higher education as follows on a 1–5 scale, where 1 was very poor and 5 was very good.

Quality of business graduates	3.28
Balance of supply of management education across specialist area	2.90
Marketing of management education courses to industry	3.00
Management education institutions' knowledge of industrial practice	2.64
Value for money of management education institutions	2.84
International perspective of management education	2.55
Value system of higher education *vis-à-vis* industry	2.51

10. Financial issues – paying for expansion

When asked for an appropriate annual amount per person to spend on developing managers, the mean response was £877. As with current expenditure, however, this figure can only be taken as a crude estimate.

Asked how the costs of increasing the provision of management education should be distributed, 54 per cent said that companies should pay the direct costs of expansion but that government should pay the infrastructure costs. 17 per cent said that companies should pay the full costs of any expansion and the same number that funding should be matched with government matching money raised from industry pound for pound. Eight per cent said that individuals should pay a substantial proportion of the costs of any external education. Only half of the respondents felt there should be more attractive tax incentives for management training and education.

EPILOGUE

The two reports, 'The Making of Managers' and 'The Making of British Managers' were published on the same day in April 1987. They produced a lot of comment in the relevant press. 'This Report (The Making of Managers), said Lord Young, the Secretary of State for Trade and Industry, 'should be read in every boardroom.' It probably was not, but a summary of it almost certainly found its way to every Personnel Manager in Britain.

As an almost immediate response the Foundation for Management Education (originally formed to create the first business schools) took it upon itself to gather together representations of industry, academia and government to consider the reports and how best to implement them. A tripartite Council was formed, the Council for Management Education and Development, under the Chairmanship of Bob Reid, Chairman of Shell UK, of FME itself and now soon to be Chairman of the British Institute of Management.

The Council has been active. It spawned working parties. One working party set about enrolling a Charter Group of leading companies and drawing up a suggested Code of Conduct or Charter to which they would be asked to subscribe. Another working party sought to follow up the recommendations in both reports for a two-tier education and to draw up criteria and curricula for the first tier. A third working party looked at the slightly older manager who would not be interested in the early educational programmes, but who needed the encouragement to develop himself or herself.

One year later substantial progress has been made in all three areas.

The Management Charter Initiative, as it has been labelled, will probably become public and official in the Autumn of 1988. The Council has gone further; it has investigated the possibility of a Royal Institute of Chartered Management with categories of Chartered Managers on the lines of the older professions, as a way of giving status and credentials to all managers of all ages, and of blending formal education with practical experience as joint prerequisites for membership.

At present, British Industry, whilst respecting the motives for such an Institute is suspicious of the bureaucratization and standardization that would be implied. Managing is a complex task, not easily defined in general terms or definitions, nor is 'the manager' any longer an easily definable route or status. Managers, it is widely felt, should be professional but not professionals, and case law not institutions still provides the best legitimacy in Britain.

There may be disagreement still about the best methods, but what is clearly evident is the new enthusiasm for, and respectability of, education for business and development for managers. It is a significant culture change which we are witnessing, well-timed to coincide with the new emphasis on enterprise. MBA courses are proliferating, are even under discussion at Oxford and Cambridge Universities, organizations are queuing up to boast of their latest initiatives, often in partnership with the Business Schools, while business recruits recite their investment in the education and development of their executives as a lure to applicants.

It is a fast-growing marketplace with demand outstripping supply. That is inevitably a recipe for experimentation, for some poor quality products and for hasty improvisation. There is a shortage, particularly, of teachers and a total lack of any mechanism for quality control. The danger is now that of disenchantment and of confusion in the new jungle of courses and programmes and initiatives. The British still have to find the right blend of the Corporate, the Academic and the Professional in their approach to Making Managers. The Reports, however, have helped to change the culture of society, to create a new climate and a new atmosphere. The old world of pragmatism and nothing else is gone forever.

BIBLIOGRAPHIES AND REFERENCES

CHAPTER 1 - REFERENCES

1. Mumford, A. and Stradling, D., 'Developing Directors: the learning process', International Management Centre at Buckingham, 1987.
    2. Revans, R., *Action Learning*, Blond and Briggs, 1980.
    3. Katz, L., 'The skills of an effective administrator', *Harvard Business Review*, Jan–Feb 1955.

CHAPTER 2 - BIBLIOGRAPHY

Japanese materials

Amaya, T., *Kore kara no noryoku kaihatsu*, Senbundo, Tokyo, 1983. (Ability development from now on.)
    Aonuma, Y., *Nihon no keieiso – sono shusshin to seikaku*, Tokyo, 1965. (Top managers in Japan: their careers and characteristics.)
    Chusho Kigyo-cho (eds), *Gijutsu Kakushin to Chusho Kigyo – Chusho Kigyo Kindaika Shingikai Hokoku*, Tsusho Sangyo, Tokyo, 1985. (Technological innovation and small and medium-sized enterprises – the report of the Deliberative Council on Modernization of Small and Medium Sized Enterprises.)
    Chusho Kigyo-cho (eds), *Showa 60 Chusho Kigyo Hakusho*, Okurasho Insatsukyoku, Tokyo, 1986. (1986 White Paper on small and medium-sized enterprises.)

Iwata, Ryushi, 'Daigaku Kyoiku to Kigyonai Kyoiku', *Keizai Hyoron*, December 1983. (University education and in-company education.)

Keiei Kikaku-Cho Kokumin Seikatsukyoku Kokumin Seikatus Chosa-ka (eds), *Zu de Miru Seikatsu Hakusho*, Doyukan, Tokyo, 1985. (Economic Planning Agency White Paper on living standards.)

Keizai Kikaku-Cho, *Keizai Yoran 1986*, Okurasho Insatsukyoku, Tokyo, 1986. (Economic Planning Agency – economic handbook, 1986.)

Nihon Sangyo Kunren Kyokai (eds), *Johoka, Haitekuka, Kokusaika ni taio suru Kigyonai Jinzai Ikusei no Genjo to kadai – Showa 60 nendo Sangyo Kunren Jissai Chosa Hokoku*, Tokyo, 1985. (Japan Industrial and Vocational Training Association: Present situation and problems for in-company human resource development to cope with the impact of information, high technology and internationalization: The Fiscal 1985 Report Industrial Training Survey Report.)

Rodo Jiho (eds), 'Minkan Kigyo ni okeru Kyoiku Kunren', *Rodo Jiho*, March 1984. (Education and training in private industry.)

Rinji Kyoiku Shingikai, *Kyoiku Kaikaku ni kansuru Dainiji Toshin*, Monbusho, Tokyo, 1986. (Special Deliberative Council on Education: Second report on education reform.)

Saito Takenori, *Gendai Nihon no Keieigaku Kyoiku*, Seibundo, Tokyo, 1977. (Contemporary Japanese business studies education.)

Shakai Tsushin Kyoiku Kyokai, *Monbusho Nintei Shakai Tshushin Kyoiku: Kaizen ni kansuru Chosa Kenkyu Hokokusho*, Monbusho, Tokyo, 1986. (Report on research survey on improvement of Ministry of Education approval (system) for correspondence course education.)

Takamiya, Susumu, *Nihon no Keieikyoiku e no Teigen*, Sangyo Noritsu Tanki Daigaku Shuppanbu, Tokyo, 1976. (Suggestions for Japanese business education.)

Tsusansho Sangyo Seisaku-kyoku Kigyo Kodo-Ka, *Sogo Keieiryoku Shihyo; Teisei Yuin no Teiryoteki Hyoka no Kokoromi*, Okurasho Insatsukyoku, Tokyo, 1986. (MITI Industrial Policy Bureau Enterprise Activity Section: General business indicators – an experiment in quantative evaluation of qualitative factor manufacturing.)

English materials

Amaya, T., *Human resource development in Japanese industry*, Japan Institute of Labour, Tokyo, 1982.

Anthony, D., 'Management education in Japan', *The Business Graduate*, January 1984.

Azumi, K., *Higher education and business recruitment in Japan*, OECD, 1982.

Coke, S., 'Wot! No business schools? Japanese graduates and major companies', *The Business Graduate*, January 1984.

Cooper, C., and Kuniya, N., 'Participative management practice and work humanisation in Japan', *Personnel Review*, 1978.

Hoshino, Y., 'Staff motivation; job mobility are keys to Japanese advance', *Sumitomo Quarterly*, Summer 1982.

Inohara, H., 'Importing managerial techniques', *Bulletin 35*, Socio-Economic Institute Sophia Univ. Japan, 1972.

Inome, K., *The education and training of industrial manpower in Japan*, World Bank Staff Working Paper No 729.

International Management Association of Japan, 'Lessons learned from Western managerial programs', *Management Japan*, Vol 7, 1974.

Kishi, T., 'The seniority system and human resources development', *Sumitomo Quarterly*, Winter 1985.

Kishi, T., 'Definition and methods of human resources development', *Sumitomo Quarterly*, Spring 1986.

Kishi, T., 'How classroom training is conducted – Part One', *Sumitomo Quarterly*, Summer 1986.

Kishi, T., 'How classroom training is conducted – Part Two', *Sumitomo Quarterly*, Autumn 1986.

Kitaya, Y., 'The age of Holonic Management', *Japan Echo*, Vol. 13, 1986.

Management and Coordination Agency, *Statistical Handbook of Japan 1986*, Japan Statistical Association, Tokyo, 1966.

Mannari, H., *The Japanese business leaders*, University of Tokyo Press, 1974.

Mano, O., 'On the development of personnel management in Japan', *Hokudai Economic Papers*, Vol 4, 1974/75.

Mano, O., 'Recent research on the Japanese personnel management system in Japan', *Hokudai Economic Papers*, Vol 9, 1979/80.

McNulty, N., *Management development programs: The world's best*, North

Holland – Elsevier, Amsterdam, 1980.

Morikawa, K., 'The development of managerial enterprise in Japan', Paper presented at Anglo-Japanese Business History Conference – LSE Business History Unit, August 1986.

Nagata, K., 'Professional education of executives: The Japanese experience', *Journal of the Mitsubishi Research Institute*, Tokyo, 1982.

Nagata, K., 'On-the-job training – a key factor of Japanese management education', *The Business Graduate*, January 1984.

Nakagawa, K., 'Japanese management in its historical perspective', Paper presented at Anglo-Japanese Business History Conference – LSE Business History Unit, August 1986.

Rehder, R., 'Education and training: have the Japanese beaten us again?', *Personnel Journal*, January 1983.

Shimada, H., 'Human resource strategies for a creative society', *Japan Echo*, Vol 13, 1986.

Shimizu, H., 'Development of management improvement techniques at Sumitomo Electric Industries', (Unpublished Paper) November 1984.

Shimizu, I., 'Japanese higher education', *The Business Graduate*, January 1984.

Subocz, V., 'Management education in Japan: extent, directions and problems', *Journal of Management Education*, Vol 3.

Sumitomo Electric Industries Training Department, *Training system, December 1984.*

Sumitomo Personnel Development and Education Department, Introduction to personnel development and education program, (Unpublished) May 1986.

Suzuki, N., 'Japanese MBAs: frontrunners to the multinationalization of Japanese business', *Journal of Management Development*, Vol 3, 1984.

Tanaka, H., 'The Japanese method of preparing today's graduate to become tomorrow's manager', *Personnel Journal*, February 1980.

Tanaka, H., 'New employee education in Japan', *Personnel Journal*, January 1981.

Tesar, G. and Suzuki, N., 'Management training programs in Japan', *The Business Graduate*, January 1984.

Tominomori, K., 'Mechanism of Japanese management and its foundation', *Hokudai Economic Papers*, Vol 9, 1981/82.

Tsuda, M., 'Study of Japanese management development practices

1', *Hitotsubashi Journal of Social Studies*, May 1977.

Tsuda, M., 'Study of Japanese management development practices 2', *Hitotsubashi Journal of Social Studies*, September 1977.

Tsuda, M., 'Study of Japanese management development practices 3', *Hitotsubashi Journal of Social Studies*, April 1978.

Tsuda, M., 'Study of Japanese management development practices 4,' *Hitotsubashi Journal of Social Studies*, July 1979.

Tung, B., *Key to Japan's economic strength: human power*, Lexington Books, Lexington, 1984.

Ueno, I., 'Sanno Institute of Business Administration: a unique institution', *The Business Graduate*, January 1984.

Yonekawa, S., 'University graduates in Japanese enterprises before the Second World War', *Business History*, Vol 26, 1984.

Yoshino, M., *Japan's managerial system*, Cambridge USA, 1968.

CHAPTER 3 – REFERENCES

1. Eurich, N.P., Corporate Classrooms: the learning business. Carnegie Foundation for the Advancement of Learning. 1985.

2. Stolzenburg, P.M. 'The changing demand for graduate management education' quoting Alexander Astin's research at UCLA in *Selections*, the Magazine of the Graduate Management Admission council, Los Angeles, Spring 1985.

3. Statistics in this section are taken from: The *Condition of Education*, National Center for Education Statistics, US Department of Education. 1987.

4. Schein, E.H., *Career Dynamics: Matching Individual and Organizational Needs*, Addison-Wesley, 1978.

5. Korn Ferry International, 'A Survey of Corporate Leaders in the Eighties', Korn Ferry International, 1987.

6. Forester, J.W., 'A new corporate design', *Industrial Management Review*, Fall 1965.

7. 'Trends in management training', Executive Development Associates, 1986.

8. 'Executive education in corporate America', Executive Knowledgeworks, 1986.

9. 'Employee training in America', *Training and Development Journal*,

July 1986.

10. *Trends in Corporate Education and Training*, Report No. 870, The Conference Board, 1985.

11. 'A world turned upside-down', Tom Peters Group, 1986.

12. Quoted in Williams, H., 'Dedication: why new management is needed', *New Management*, Vol. 1, Spring 1983.

CHAPTER 4 - BIBLIOGRAPHY

Richard Whitley, Alan Thomas and Jane Marceau, *Masters of business? Business schools in France and Britain*, Tavistock Publications, 1981.

Henri Tézanas du Montcel, *L'Université peut mieux faire*, Seuil, Paris, 1985.

Laurent Schwartz, *Pour sauver l'Université*, Seuil, Paris, 1983.

Jean-Michel Gaillard, *Tu seras président, mon fils*, Ramsay, Paris, 1987.

Dominique Xardel, *Les Managers*, Grasset, Paris, 1978.

Yves Cannac and La Cegos, *La bataille de la compétence*, Editions Hommes et Techniques, Paris, 1985.

Formation professionnelle, Document Annexe, Projet de Loi de Finances pour 1986, Imprimerie Nationale, Paris, 1985.

La formation professionnelle continue, Chambre de Commerce et d'Industrie de Paris, Paris, 1985.

Enquête sur l'emploi de 1985, INSEE, Paris, 1985.

Recensement général de la population de 1982, INSEE, Paris.

Statistique de la formation professionnelle continue financée par les entreprises 1983–4, CEREQ, Paris, 1985.

Jean-Paul Gehin and Jean-François Germe, *Formation continue et PME*, CEREQ, 1985.

Marc Maurice, François Sellier, Jean-Jacques Silvestre, *Politique d'éducation et organisation industrielle en France et en Allemagne*, PUF, Paris, 1982.

Guy Le Boterf, *Où va la formation des cadres?*' Editions d'Organisation, Paris, 1984.

Yves Delamotte, *Les cadres des entreprises dans un monde en mutation*, Bureau International du Travail, Geneva, 1986.

Josiane Serre, *Rapport sur l'enseignement supérieur au niveau des classes préparatoires*', Paris, 1985.

Vincens, J., *Les formations élitistes et l'évolution de l'enseignement supérieur*, Centre d'Études Juridiques et Economiques de l'Emploi, Note No. 39, May 1986.

Commissariat Général du Plan, 'Développer la formation en enteprises', Documentation Française, Paris, 1985.

Sarfaty, D., and Théophile, J., *La Formation Continue*, Cahiers Enseignment et Gestion, Winter 1984–5.

CHAPTER 5 - REFERENCES

1. Witte, E., Kallmann, A., and Sachs, G., *Führungskräfte der Wirtschaft*, Poeschel, 1980, p. 1.

2. Fores, M., Sorge, A., and Lawrence, P., 'Why Germany produces better' in *Management Today*, November 1978, p. 87.

3. *Ibid.*, p. 88.

4. Purdie, E., *A History of German Literature*, Blackwood, 1959, p. 311.

5. *Grund-und Strukturdaten, 1984/85*, Der Bundesminister für Bildung und Wissenschaft, p. 180.

6. *Bildung und Wissenschaft*, Inter Nationes, No. 9–10, 1987,

7. *Competence and Competition*, Institute of Manpower Services, 1984, p. 18.

8. *Bildung und Wissenschaft*, Inter Nationes, No. 3–4, 1986, p. 5.

9. Prais, S.J., and Wagner, K., 'Schooling standards in England and Germany: some summary comparisons bearing on economic performance', in *National Institute Economic Review*, May 1985, p. 55.

10. *Bildung und Wissenschaft*, Inter Nationes, No. 3–4, 1986, p. 5.

11. Prais, S.J., and Wagner, K., *op. cit., loc. cit.*

12. *Bildung und Wissenschaft*, Inter Nationes, No. 3–4, 1986, p.5.

13. Prais, S.J., and Wagner, K., *op. cit., loc. cit.*

14. *Grund-und Strukturdaten, 1984/85*, Der Bundesminister für Bildung und Wissenschaft, p. 56.

15. Staufenbiel, J.E., *Berufsplanung für den Management-Nachwuchs*, iba, 1981, p. 62.

16. Heidensohn, K., *Fachhochschulen and Polytechnics*, Bristol, 1984, p. 8.

17. *Grund- und Strukturdaten, 1984/85*, Der Bundesminister für Bildung und Wissenschaft, p. 116.

18. *Ibid.*, p. 132.

19. Klein, R., 'Klasse aus der Provinz', in *Manager-Magazin*, No. 1, 1986, p. 123.

20. *Grund- und Strukturdaten, 1984/85*, Der Bundesminister für Bildung und Wissenschaft, p. 111.

21. *Ibid.*, p. 126.

22. Locke, R.R., 'Business education in Germany: past systems and current practice', in *Business History Review*, Harvard, Summer 1985, p. 244.

23. *Grund- und Strukturdaten, 1984/85*, Der Bundesminister für Bildung und Wissenschaft, p. 160.

24. Staufenbiel, J.E., *op. cit.*, p. 80.

25. *Ibid.*, p. 80.

26. *Informationsdienst des Instituts der deutschen Wirtschaft*, No. 21, 1985, p. 6.

27. *Ibid.*, p. 6.

28. Locke, R.R., *op. cit.*, p. 234.

29. H. Thorburg, 'Die Deutschen machen sich rar', in *Manager-Magazin*, No. 10, 1985, p. 200.

30. von Plüskow, H-J., 'Königsweg', in *Capital*, December 1987, p. 287.

31. *Abschlußbericht zum Forschungsprojekt 'Studienreform und Berufspraxisbezug'*, Bundesvereinigung der deutschen Arbeitgeberverbände/Institut für Sozial- und Bildungspolitik Hamburg e.V., July 1981, pp. 17–18.

32. Staufenbiel, J.E., *op. cit.*, p. 86.

33. *Ibid.*, p. 46.

34. *30 Jahre Baden-Badener Unternehmergespräche*, Gesellschaft zur Förderung des Unternehmernachwuchses e.V. und Deutsches Institut zur Förderung des industriellen Führungsnachwuchses, Cologne, 1985, p. 5.

35. *Westerham 86*, Industrie und Handelskammer für München und Oberbayern, Munich, 1986, pp. 4–5.

36. *Tätigkeitsbericht 1984/85*, Bildungswerk der Bayerischen Wirtschaft, e.V., Munich, 1985, p. 5.

37. *Bildung und Wissenschaft*, Inter Nationes, No. 11–12, 1987, p. 18.

38. *Ibid.*, p. 19.

39. *Ibid.*, p. 18.

40. Böhler, W., *Betriebliche Weiterbildung und Bildungsurlaub*, Centainerius, 1984, p. 8.

41. *Frauen als Führungskräfte in der Wirtschaft*, FIDA, Hamburg, 1986, p. 5.

42. *Grund- und Strukturdaten 1984/85*, Der Bundesminister für Bildung und Wissenschaft, p. 158.

43. *Frauen als Führungskräfte in der Wirtschaft*, FIDA, Hamburg, 1986.

44. *Ibid.*, p. 5.

45. *Ibid.*, p. 5.

46. *Ibid.*, p. 13.

47. *Ibid.*, pp. 14–15.

48. *Ibid.*, p. 15.

49. *Ibid.*, p. 53.

50. Franke, H., 'Der Arbeitsmarkt für Führungskräfte bis zum Jahre 2000', in *Stellenjournal*, November 1984, p. 3.

51. *Der Spiegel*, No. 25, 1986, p. 105.

52. 'Strenge Hierarchie bei den Bezügen', in *Manager-Magazin*, No. 10, 1985, p. 56.

53. Kienbaum, J., and von Landsberg, G., *Erfolgsmerkmale von Führungskräften*, Cologne, 1987, p. 39.

54. *Der Spiegel*, No. 20, 1985, p. 40.

55. Kienbaum, J., and von Landsberg, G., *op. cit.*, pp. 38–9.

56. *Bildung und Wissenschaft*, Inter Nationes, No. 11–12, 1987,

57. Franke, H., *op. cit.*, *loc. cit.*

58. *Ibid.*, p. 4.

59. *Ibid.*, p. 4.

60. Nussbaum, B., *The World after Oil*, New York, 1983.

61. *Ibid.*, p. 83.

62. *Ibid.*, p. 83–4.

63. *Der Spiegel*, No. 43, 1983, pp. 167–71.

64. *Der Spiegel*, No. 52, 1983, pp. 19–29.

65. *Der Spiegel*, No. 44, 1985, pp. 43–5.

66. Nussbaum, B., *op. cit.*, p. 43.

67. *Ibid.*, p. 90.

68. *The Economist*, November 8, 1986, p. 67.

69. *Ibid.*, p. 67.

70. *Ibid.*, p. 68.

71. Klein, R., and Lenz, B., 'Die Brücke zum Aufstieg', in *Manager-Magazin*, No. 3, 1987, p. 229.

72. Tümmers, H.J., *Von der Volkswirtschaft zur Weltwirtschaft*,

Reutlingen, 1987, p. 13.
  73. *Ibid.*, p. 13.
  74. 'Der Nachwuchs strebt in die USA', in *Manager-Magazin*, No. 3, 1987, p. 232.
  75. *Ibid.*, p. 232.

CHAPTER 5 - BIBLIOGRAPHY

Ambrosius, G., *Der Staat als Unternehmer*, Göttingen, 1984.
  Burtenshaw, D., *The Economic Geography of Germany*, London, 1984.
  Carl, M., and Zahn, P., *The German Private Limited Company*, London, 1982.
  Childs, D., and Johnson, J., *West Germany – Politics and Society*, London, 1981.
  Conradt, D.P., *The German Polity*, New York, 1978.
  Cullingford, E.C.M., *Trade Unions in Germany*, London, 1976.
  Drucker, P., *The Age of Discontinuity*, London, 1969.
  Engelmann, B., *Meine Freunde die Manager*, Munich, 1969.
  Grosser, A., *Germany in Our Time*, Harmondsworth, 1970.
  Hübner, E., and Rolfs, H-H., *Jahrbuch der Bundesrepublik Deutschland 1986/87*, Munich, 1986.
  Jäkel, E., and Junge, W., *Die deutschen Industrie- und Handelskammern und der Deutsche Industrie- und Handelstag*, Düsseldorf, 1978.
  Kloss, G., *West Germany – An Introduction*, London, 1976.
  Lawrence, P., *Managers and Management in West Germany*, London, 1980.
  Lutz, B., and Kammerer, G., *Das Ende des graduierten Ingenieurs*, Frankfurt, 1975.
  Owen-Smith, E., *The West German Economy*, London, 1983.
  Panic, M., *The UK and West German Manufacturing Industry, 1954–72*, London, 1973.
  Pross, H., and Boetticher, K. *Manager des Kapitalismus*, Frankfurt, 1971.
  Sontheimer, K., *The Government and Politics of West Germany*, London, 1972.
  Stewart, R., *Contrasts in Management*, Maidenhead, 1976.
  Wallraff, G., *Industrie-Reportagen*, Reinbek bei Hamburg, 1970.

Weinshall, T.D., *Culture and Management*, Harmondsworth, 1977.
Witte, E., and Bronner, R., *Die Leitenden Angestellten*, Munich, 1975.

CHAPTER 6 – REFERENCES

1. Ascher, K., *Management Training in Large UK Business Organizations*, Harbridge House, 1983.
2. Mangham, I.L., and Silver, M.S., *Management training – content and practice*, ESPC & DTI, 1986.
3. Constable, J., and McCormick, R., *The Making of British Managers*, BIM, 1987.

BIBLIOGRAPHY

Adams, M., and Meadows, P., 'The changing graduate labour market', *Employment Gazette*, September 1985.
Association of Management Education Centres, *Improving the effectiveness of British management*, Background paper prepared by the Executive, 30 June 1986.
Ascher, K., 'Mastering the business graduate', *Personnel Management*, January 1986.
Ashton, D., (Ed), *Management Bibliographies and Review*, Vol. 4, MCB, Bradford, 1978.
Ball, R.J., 'Management education in the United Kingdom', *London Business School Journal*, Summer 1983.
Ball, R.J., 'A business school view of management education', *Personnel Management*, August 1984.
Bernthal, W., 'Matching German culture and management style: a book review essay', *Academy of Management Review*, January 1978.
Betts, P., 'Grande école goes English', *Financial Times, 19 May 1986*.
Bickerstaffe, G., *Crisis of Confidence in the Business School*, International Management, August 1981.
BIM, *Business School Programmes – the Requirements of British Manufacturing Industry*, BIM, 1971.
CBI, *Change to Succeed – a Consultation Document*, 1985.
Commission of the European Communities and European

Foundation for Management Development, *Management education in the European Community*, 1976.

Department of Education and Science, *Statistical Bulletins 9/84, 9/85, 11/85, 7/86, 13/85*, Education Statistics for the UK, 1985.

Dickerman, A., *Training Japanese Managers*, Praeger Press, New York, 1975.

Dixon, M., 'Management education and training', *Financial Times*, 30 September 1985.

Eglin, R., 'That ole-style boss just keeps bumbling along', *Sunday Times*, 1 June 1986.

Fores, M., Lawrence, P., and Sorve, A., 'Germany's front line force', *Management Today*, March 1978.

Forrester, P., *A Study of the Practical Use of the MBA, BIM, 1984.*

Garrison, T., R., *Business and Management Education in France*, Thames Valley Regional Management Centre, 1976.

Granick, D., 'International differences in executive reward systems: extent, explanation and significance', *Columbia Journal of World Business*, Summer 1978.

Hayes, C., Anderson, A., and Fond, N., 'International competition and the role of competence', *Personnel Management*, September 1984.

Holland, G., 'Excellence in industry', Summary of talk at BIM Conference, 11 February 1986.

Horovitz, J., 'The frontier of management European style', *Vision*, January 1979.

Industrial Society, *Survey of Training Costs*, New Series No. 1, 1985.

Jarratt, A., 'British manufacturing – problem or opportunity', Henry Ford II Scholar Award Lecture at Cranfield School of Management, 14 May 1986.

Kakabadse, A., 'How bosses fail in "people skills"', *Sunday Times*, 27 April 1986.

Kempner, T., 'Education for management in five countries: myth and reality', *Journal of General Management*, Winter 1983/84.

Kloss, G., *West Germany: an Introduction*, Macmillan, 1976.

Knox, D., 'Oiling the wheels of complacency', *Management Accounting*, March 1986.

Leggatt, T., *The Training of British Managers: a Study of Need and Demand*, HMSO, 1972.

Locke, R.R., 'Business education in Germany: post systems and current practice', *Business History Review 59*, Summer 1985.

Lupton, T., *Business Schools in the 80s and Beyond*, Working Paper Series No. 49, Manchester Business School, 1980.

Lupton, T., *The Structure and Functions of Business Schools in the 80s*, Working Paper Series No. 68, Manchester Business School, 1981.

McNay, I., *European management education: history, typologies and national structures*, Management Education and Development 4, 1973.

McDougall, R., *Review of Management Education in the United Kingdom*, European Foundation for Management Development, 1976.

Mant, A., *The Experienced Manager – a Major Resource*, BIM, 1969.

Margerison, C., and Kakabadse, A., 'What management development means for American CEO', *Journal of Management Development*, 4, 5, 1985.

Milborrow, G. and Webb, I., 'Management training in the context of the company', Paper to BIM, January 1986.

MSC and NEDO, *A Challenge to Complacency: Changing Attitudes to Training*, MSC, 1985.

Nagata, K., 'Professional education of executives: the Japanese experience', *Journal of Mitsubishi Research Institute*, No. 10, 1981.

NEDO and MSC, *Competence and Competition – Training and Education in the Federal Republic of Germany, the United States and Japan*, NEDO, 1984.

Newman, N., 'The MBA credibility gap', *Management Today*, December 1981.

Osbaldeston, M., and Warner, A., 'In search of excellence in business schools', *Personnel Management*, March 1985.

Owen, T., *Business School Programmes – the requirement of British manufacturing industry*, British Institute of Management, 1970.

Prais, S., 'Vocational qualifications of the labour force in Britain and Germany', *National Institute Economic Review*, November 1981.

Prais, S., and Wagner, K., 'Some practical aspects of human capital investment: training standards in five occupations in Britain and Germany', *National Institute Economic Review*, August 1983.

Prais, S., and Wagner, K., 'School standards in England and Germany: some summary comparisons bearing on economic performance', *National Institute Economic Review*, May 1985.

Prais, S., and Steadman, H., 'Vocational training in France and Britain: the building trades', *National Institute Economic Review*, May 1986.

Prins, D., Seeringer W., and Wilpert, B., *Business Education and the EEC*

Report on German Fachhochschulen, International Institute of Management, Berlin, 1972.

Rose, H., *Management Education in the 1970s*, HMSO, 1970.

Sasaki, N., *Management and Industrial Structure in Japan*, Pergamon Press, 1981.

Saussois, J.M., *French Research in Cadres: Results and Perspectives*, International Studies of Management and Organization, Spring 1984.

Taylor, D., 'Learning from Japan', Review of Conference, DE Work Research Unit, 19/20 December 1983.

Wakabayashi, M., *Management Career Progress in a Japanese Organization*, UMI Research Press, Ann Arbor, Michigan, 1980.

Warner, M., 'Industrialization, management education and training systems: a comparative analysis', *Journal of Management Studies*, Winter 1986/87.

Whitely, R., Thomas, A., and Marceau, J., *Masters of Business*, Tavistock, 1981.

Willatt, N., 'The French school of management', *Management Today*, August 1979.

Willatt, N., 'Europe's new management medicine', *Management Today*, October 1972.

INDEX

Page numbers in **bold type** refer to the list of references at the end of the book.